FASHION DESIGN

A Technical Foundation

Women's Wear Pattern Cutting

by Tanya Dove

FASHION DESIGN

A CIP catalogue record for this title is available from the British Library.

ISBN 978 1 84963 471 7

www.austinmacauley.com

First Published (2013)
Austin Macauley Publishers Ltd.
25 Canada Square
Canary Wharf
London
E14 5LB

Printed and Bound in Great Britain

"To all the teachers and guides who have crossed my path,
I thank you.

To all the students I have taught I thank you too,
for all the pattern making handouts I provided to you
are now inside
A Technical Foundation.

To all the designers this book will guide in the future, enjoy".

Tanya Dove - Designer, Creator, Author

CONTENTS

Introduction

FASHION DESIGN: A Technical Foundation

A Technical Foundation is a women's wear pattern-cutting guide for all fashion designers. From aspiring students, to a fashion design lecturer's reference material, and designers alike. It provides detailed construction information for garment blocks that are used within fashion design.

To create collections, whether model size for catwalk shows and photo shoots, or an individual's size, garment blocks are always used and adapted into the chosen design. *A Technical Foundation* takes you through the creation of these blocks, which can then be used and adapted repeatedly. It is a foundation of pattern cutting as it shows you how to create the blocks, not individual garment designs.

A Technical Foundation is divided into twenty-one chapters of garment blocks, components and finishing used in garment construction. Each chapter has detailed information and clear technical pictures showing how to construct the different garment blocks and take them to plans and patterns.

The garment construction chapters provide a range of different blocks to be used to construct the specific garment – for a skirt there is a straight skirt, full skirt, circle skirt and pencil skirt. These blocks can then be used at the designer's discretion to design his or her own range. Each garment section covers a multitude of garment blocks, which makes adapting different blocks into individual designs that much easier as *A Technical Foundation* covers a choice of blocks for each garment to work from.

The garment component chapters show in detail how to construct different garment components, from adding fullness into clothing - the four varieties of pleats, godets and gathers. Different ways to finish the waistline and neckline, sleeve shapes, hoods, collars, plackets, cuffs to front openings and different styles of pockets.

The chapters have been designed in an order of simplicity at the beginning, and the technical aspect of pattern cutting getting more complex throughout the book. Ranging from skirt and trouser blocks through to tailoring, contouring and jersey wear blocks. With each garment and component in different chapters *A Technical Foundation* has been designed in a way for the designers to evolve through the book reaching a level of understanding and practice, to then have the technical skills to design their own collections. There are also technically illustrated sample designs to show the type of garments that the different blocks can create.

The measurements quoted for all pattern making are a UK size 10. (Approximately an EU 34 and a US size 6). The measurements have been decided from an analysis of retailers and their sizing charts across the globe. There is no definitive sizing chart, many retailers adjusting their sizing to suit the age group of their customers. There is a column on the sizing chart for the designers to write their chosen measurements. All construction measurements quoted throughout the book also have the formula to obtain such measurement, which enables changing the size of the blocks easier for the designer.

A Technical Foundation also shows detailed technical specification templates to enable the designers to draw their designs in detail. It has a specific chapter for costing garments and specification sheets to pass the pattern onto a factory or tailor to make the designs. The grading chapter shows a grading size chart of how to change garment sizes, with detailed information on pivot grading.

The final chapter, Fabrics, gives information on how to cut out fabric and the different fabric qualities. There are many choices of fabrics available to use within fashion design, from natural fibres like cotton, wool, silk and linen to man made and mixed fibre fabrics. The right fabric for garment design depends on the design itself. The same pattern can be used with different fabrics but the finish look will be different. Fluid light fabrics will drape down the body, where as firmer heavier fabrics will hang over the body. The fibres charts give a description of some different types of natural and manufactured fabrics available.

A Technical Foundation

by Tanya Dove

1. Information

FASHION DESIGN

Measurement Size Chart

The measurement size chart is a guide on body measurements for UK size 10, 12 and 14.

The measurements have been compiled by an analysis of top high street retailers in the UK and the way they size their clothing. There is no definitive size chart across the UK, or indeed across the globe for garment sizes. Many stores choosing to adapt their size towards their customer, whereby teenage stores sizing has smaller measurements for a size 10, and mature clothing stores have larger measurements for a size 10. The main difference between size 10 and 12 is the bust, waist and hip measurement where a 5cm grade (size difference) is used. This still remains relatively standard across the industry.

There is a column for you to add in your own size chart, whether it be your own measurements or your idealistic body size.

Measurement	SIZE in CM			
	UK 10	UK 12	UK 14	Your Size
BL - Bust line - approx 24cm down from H.P.S.	83	87	93	
WL - Waist line - 41cm down from centre back neck	67	72	77	
HL - Hip line - Low hip is 20cm down from WL	90	95	100	
CBL - centre back length - from centre back neck	43	43.6	44.2	
Waist to floor length	100	101	102	
Waist to knee	55	55.5	56	
S - shoulder - total measurement	40	41.2	42.4	
Shoulder - one side	12	12.3	12.6	
Neck size	35.6	37.1	38.6	
XB - Back width - measure 11cm down from BC Neck	33.5	34.7	35.9	
XF - Chest - measure 12cm down from H.P.S	31	32.2	33.4	
Bust dart width	6	6.6	7.2	
Bust dart length at side seam position	10	10.9	11.8	
Front waist dart width	3	3	3	
Front waist dart length - WL to finish	10	10	10	
Back waist dart width	3	3	3	
Back waist dart length - WL to finish	14	14	14	
Back neck opening - fitted neckline	14	14.6	15.2	
Front neck drop - measure from H.P.S.	8	8.2	8.4	
Armhole depth	20	20.3	20.6	
BR - Body rise - from WL	27	27.7	28.4	
Knee	32	33.6	35.2	
Ankle	20.4	21	21.6	
Sleeve length	58	58.5	59	
Bicep - measure 2.5cm down from armhole	26.4	28	29.6	
Elbow	22	23	24	
Wrist	15.5	16	16.5	

FASHION DESIGN

Body Measurements

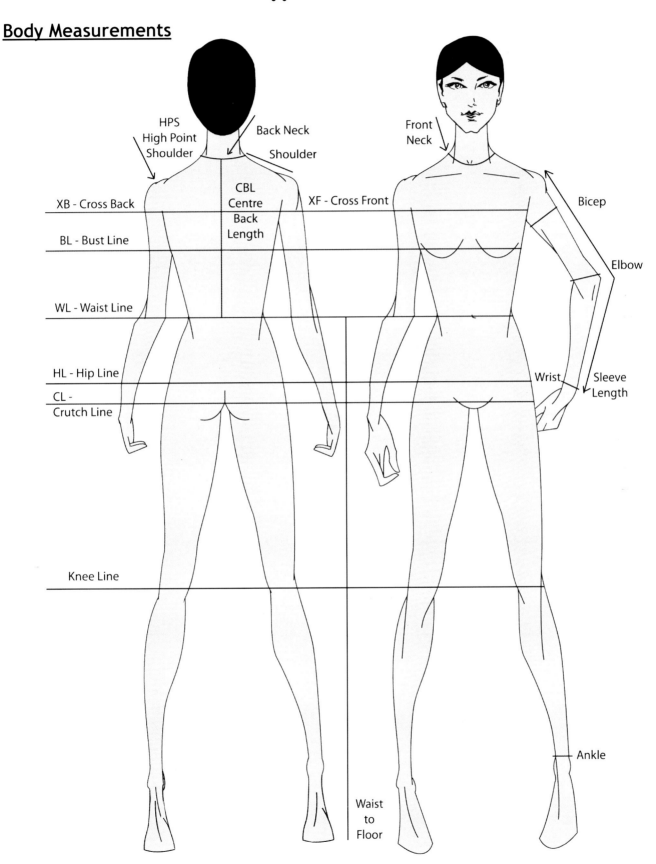

HPS
High Point
Shoulder

Back Neck

Shoulder

Front
Neck

XB - Cross Back

CBL
Centre
Back
Length

XF - Cross Front

Bicep

BL - Bust Line

Elbow

WL - Waist Line

HL - Hip Line

CL -
Crutch Line

Wrist

Sleeve
Length

Knee Line

Ankle

Waist
to
Floor

FASHION DESIGN

Abbreviations Index

Abbreviations on patterns are used all across industry to save time and space in writing the full wording. They are written on blocks, plans and patterns. Below is a chart of some key abbreviations. Depending on design, would depend on what ones you would use within your pattern construction.

CB	Centre Back
CF	Centre Front
SB	Side Back
SF	Side Front
SS	Side Seam
BL	Bust Line
WL	Waist Line
HL	Hip Line
CL	Crutch Line
CBL	Centre Back Length
HPS	High Point Shoulder
XF	Cross Front
XB	Cross Back
S	Shoulder
AD	Armhole Depth
NL	Neckline

Pattern Making Tools

1. Fine liner pencil – 0.5 lead size
2. Ruler – A pattern master ruler has straight and curved edges and a right angle. It is the only ruler required for pattern making.
3. Tape measure
4. Paper scissors
5. Notchers – notchers are used on pattern pieces to mark specific points to make sewing easier.

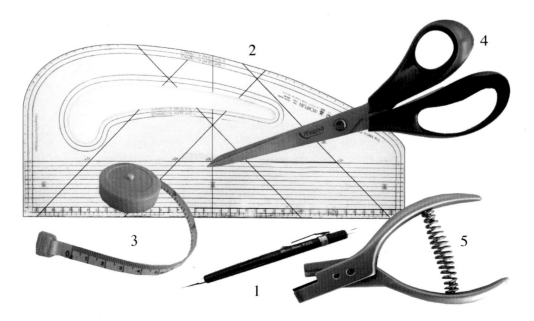

FASHION DESIGN

Ease

Ease = ease of movement. When a garment block is made with measurements there is no allowance to allow you to move and feel comfortable in the clothes. EASE is always added into all blocks as below:-

BL - Bust Line ease = 4cm (to help you breathe)
WL - Waist Line ease = 2cm (to allow for food)
HL - Hip Line ease = 4cm (so you can sit down)

The ease above is the standard industry amount. However for some fitted styles less ease can be added to achieve the finished look. I.E. A pencil skirt could have less ease at the hip, a corset has no ease to mould to the body.

Seam and Hem allowances

Seams

Seam allowances are added onto pattern pieces to allow you to sew them together. Your pattern is made from measurements that fit the body with ease of movement. Seams allow these pieces to be stitched together. Without them, the garment will be too small. The industry standard for seams is 1cm. Larger seams are used by more expensive retailers, and predominantly on tailoring - 1.5cm or 2cm seam. The most commonly used seams are:-

Straight seam is 1cm seam allowance when the seam is stitched and over locked. Over locking either together or separate and press the seam open.

Flat felled seam - this seam is used traditionally for casual clothing, jeans, casual jackets which do not have lining, casual trousers. It is also used on men's tailored shirts. 1.5cm seam allowance is used. Sewn as 1.5cm one side is cut to 0.5cm, the other folded at 0.5cm and stitched in place at 1cm finish.

Straight Seam

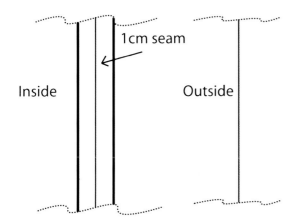

Flat Felled Seam

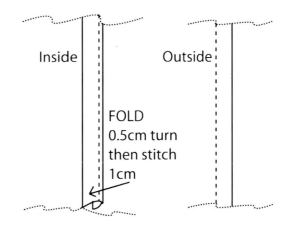

FASH✂ON DESIGN

French seam – using 1cm seam allowance you sew the right sides together first using 0.3cm seam allowance, trim, press and then sew the seam again using 0.5cm seam allowance. These are generally used on fine fabrics and eveningwear as it gives a neat small seam on the inside.

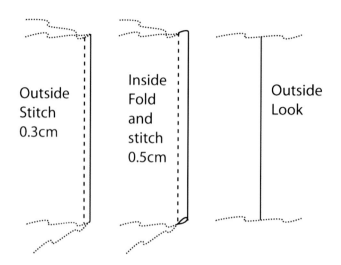

Outside Stitch 0.3cm

Inside Fold and stitch 0.5cm

Outside Look

Hems

A hem is an open edge – the bottom of a garment and sleeves.
The most common hems are:-

2cm hem allowance is used when you double turn 1cm the hem and topstitch down.

1cm hem allowance is used for a double turn 0.5cm – a 'pin' hem. This is used for fine fabrics on dress and skirt hems.

A 3-4cm hem allowance is used when you hand sew a hem. This is used for wool's and tailored garments. It is a more expensive way of finishing a garment. The top edge of the hem can either be overlocked or bound (binding is a more expensive finish).

Notches

A notch is a small indentation made on the pattern pieces and cut into the fabric. 'Notchers' are used on patterns and a small cut of 3mm in length is made on the fabric when it is cut.

Notches are marked on blocks and cut out with notchers on patterns. They are an 'aid' for when the garment is sewn. Hipline and waistline are always notched. When making a garment with panels back to back has two notches, front to front has one notch. Back to front has just one notch. 1cm seam
allowance is never notched, but bigger seam allowances do have notches. Hemline is notched when it is not 1cm. Notched are used to make sewing easier so are always used when seam lines are curved. Long seam's are notched approximately half way.

Darts

Pattern blocks have bust darts and waist darts. This is to take the 2D pattern pieces and create 3D garments to fit the human form. They are used to create shaping to fit the body where our bodies contour in and out.

Darts can be moved into panel lines so that there is no visible dart. They are rarely used as a design details. A dart is the shape of a 'V'. Where the lines of the dart are angled to the point where the excess fabric needs to be removed.

Waist darts are placed around the 3D waistline to distribute where the extra fabric is taken out. Side seams already have shape, darts split the front and back sections in half from centre to side, taking out the excess evenly. Waist darts can be moved along the waistline, but the original position gives the best distribution. Bust darts should always point towards the bust point to create the best fit.

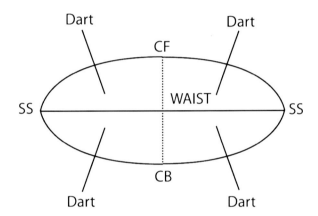

Drill Holes

A drill hole is a mark that is made on a plan, pattern and transferred onto the fabric when cutting. They are used for pockets and details that are inside a pattern piece I.E. not on an edge where you can do a notch. The position is marked accurately on the plan and pattern however on the fabric it is best marked 3mm down and 3mm across from the actual position.

Grain Lines

Grain lines are always drawn on all blocks, plans and pattern pieces. These show the direction in which the fabric is to be cut out. On blocks the grain line is drawn as the straight grain, parallel to the selvedge of the fabric. For plans and patterns the grain line depends on the garment design. The grain line is drawn as a straight line with information written down the length. The purpose of this is for the cutter to know how to cut the fabric from the pattern. It is important to ensure grain lines are
perfectly straight otherwise the fabric could be cut out wrong. This would be "off grain". Fabric is very sensitive when cut and if it is cut off grain it could cause the seams to not be smooth and the fabric to not hang down the body correctly. This is called roping.

FASHION DESIGN

Straight Grain - the selvedge is the edge of the fabric, which is naturally finished when made. The grain line follows this line down the length of the fabric (not the edge which has been cut when the fabric was purchased).

Cross Grain is when you cut at a right angle to the grain line. This would be cutting along the edge which has been cut when purchased. Only some fabrics can be cut out cross grain - these tend to be stable fabrics which do not have much natural stretch. Cross grain cutting is also used for design
detailing if the fabric is for example a stripe.

Bias Grain - when pattern pieces are cut at a 45 degree angle. This is where the fabric has the most amount of natural stretch. Bias cut garments cling more to the body, depending on the fabric they can completely hug the body. Chiffon is a fine fabric that works well for bias cut garments, where less darts or no darts are required to achieve a close fit.

Grain Line Information

PATTERN PIECE NAME	CUT INFORMATION	PATTERN NAME
YOUR NAME		SIZE

Grain Lines Diagram

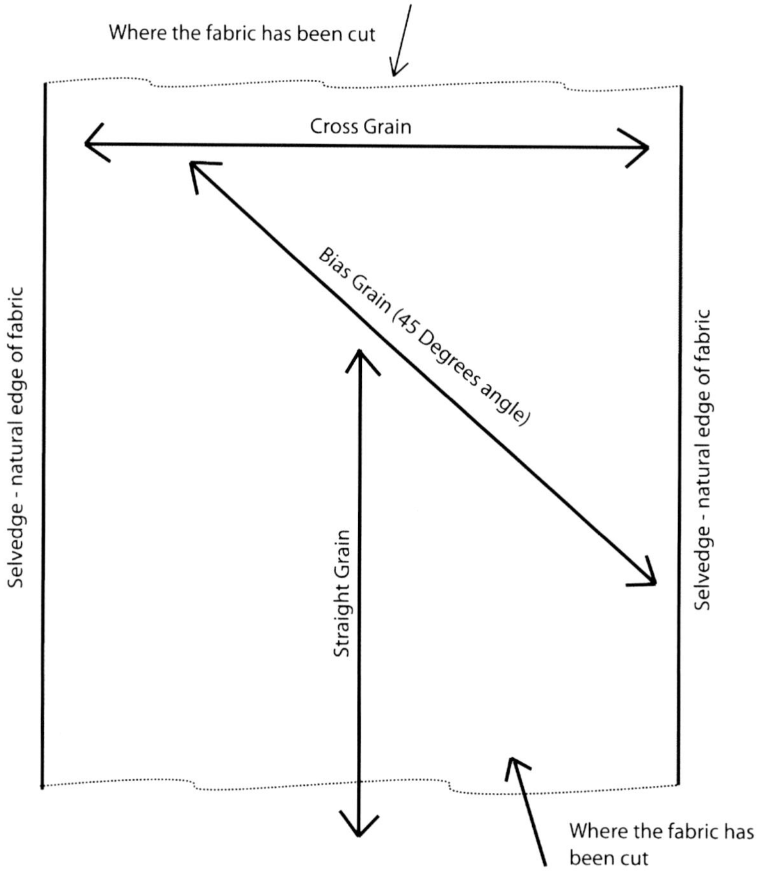

Zipper Openings

An opening on a skirt or trousers needs to finish 18cm below the waistline to enable you to get the garment over your hips. If you reduce the waist height (to make low waisted) you need to use a shorter zipper. Zips do not need to come any lower than 18cm below the waistline. A notch mark is used to show where the zipper needs to end. This is applicable for side seam and front and back openings. When a zipper is used at the side seam it is always sewn on the left side of the body – for all garments.

When choosing a zipper for your garment it is advisable to select one that is a suitable thickness and weight for the fabric you are going to use. If the zipper is too thin and light it will not be strong enough for repeated use. If the zipper is too heavy it might make the fabric drag down with the weight of the zip.

Regular Zipper

This is the zipper where you can see the zip, the "teeth". Used in trousers for the centre front fly opening. There are now many styles of regular zippers with different coloured teeth, metal, plastic and diamante style embellishments on the teeth. It opens one end only with the zipper pulley. There are many types of zipper pulleys also. This zipper is best used when you want to see the zip, or where the zip is covered by a stand.

Invisible Zipper

This zipper has the teeth on the inside so there is no visible zipper on the outside. Mainly used in dresses and skirts, sewn on the left side seam so it cannot be seen at all. It works well for fine fabrics, as the zipper is more delicate than a regular zip.

Open Ended Zipper

This zip opens both ends and is used in jackets, coats and garments where you need (or want) to open the garment up completely. The same as a regular zipper, there are many choices of open-ended zippers available. These tend to be heavier zips, and are commonly seen in casual wear and outerwear.

Interfacing

Interfacing is used to hold the shape and create a nice finish – waistline, armholes, necklines (with facings). It is cut 3mm smaller around all sides of the pattern piece. There are different weights of interfacing. You should choose a weight suitable for the fabric – ie silk satin would need lightweight, wool would need a heavier interfacing. If you are trying to create a 'stiff' form, i.e. a stand up stiff coat collar then use a very heavy interfacing. Alternatively you can hand baste canvas around the fabric to give it extra weight without stiffness.

FASHION DESIGN

2. SKIRTS

To begin making clothes you need to follow the pattern making steps = Block to Plan to Pattern

Blocks - these are basic styles made from measurements. They are used in industry as a base to create designs. Blocks do not have seam or hem allowances. Blocks are made in the basic garment categories:- Skirt, Bodice, Trouser, Jumpsuit, Jacket, Coat block etc.

Plans - a plan is made by tracing round your block and adapting it into your own style. A plan is a map of your new style. Always keep the waistline and hipline on the plan in the same position for front and back to ensure the length of your designs are correct. The lines of your new design should be drawn over the top of the basic block. Some lines will overlap depending on the designs. Different panels in the new design should be highlighted to make it easier to trace off the pattern. Plan's are never cut up. They are used for reference in case there is any design or fitting issues once the garment is made. Plan's do not have seam or hem allowances. Written information on a plan would be abreviations and the pattern name for reference.

Patterns - to make a pattern you trace off each individual piece of the plan adding on seam allowance and hem allowance. Written content on a plan consists of the pattern piece information. Grain lines are drawn on each pattern piece. Information and notches on pattern pieces are very important for when you sew the garment together.

Skirt lengths

Micro Mini	35cm
Short	40cm
Above knee	50cm
On Knee	55cm
Under Knee	60cm
Mid Calf	70cm
Ankle	100cm

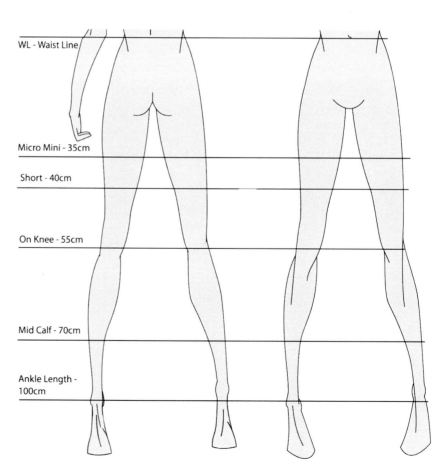

WL - Waist Line

Micro Mini - 35cm

Short - 40cm

On Knee - 55cm

Mid Calf - 70cm

Ankle Length - 100cm

FASHION DESIGN

Skirt Block Construction

BACK	SIZE 10 MEASUREMENTS
1 - 2	Skirt length - WL to Knee = 55cm
1 - 3	WL to HL = 20cm - square across points 1,2,3 to the right - Mark as CB
3 - 4	¼ hip plus 1cm ease = (1/4 of 90cm = 22.5+1cm = 23.5cm)
2 - 5	Same as 3 - 4 = 23.5cm
5 - 6	Connect 4 - 5 and continue 2cm UP from WL = point 6
1 - 7	Back princess line = 7.5cm
7 - 8	Back dart = 3cm
7 - 9	Half back dart = 9cm - square down to HL and mark point 10
9 - 11	Back dart length = 14cm. Connect 11 to 7 and 11 to 8
8 - 6	Connect with a straight line
1 - 12	¼ waist + 3cm dart + 0.5cm ease (16.75+3+0.5 = 20.25cm)
8 - 12	Join with a curved line
4 - 12	Join with a curved line

FRONT	SIZE 10 MEASUREMENTS
4 - 15	¼ hip plus 1cm ease = 23.5cm
5 - 13	Same as 4 - 45 = ¼ hip plus 1cm ease = 23.5cm
13 - 14	Connect 13 to 15 and continue line to WL - extend by 0.8cm - Mark as CF
14 - 16	Front princess line = 8cm
16 - 17	Front dart = 2.5cm
17 - 18	Half front dart = 1.25cm - square down to hipline - Mark point 19
18 - 20	Front dart length = 10cm
17 - 6	Join with a straight line
14 - 21	¼ waist + 2.5cm dart + 0.5cm ease (16.75+2.5+0.5 = 19.75cm)
17 - 21	Join with a curved line
4 - 21	Join with a curved line

Skirt Block Construction

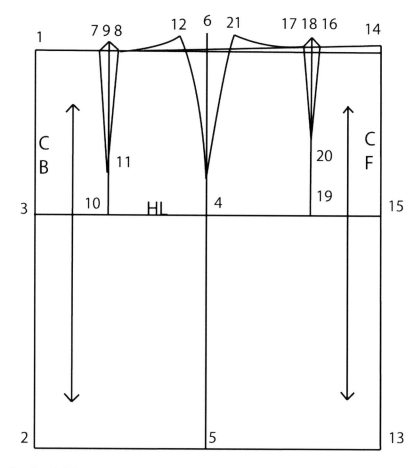

Skirt Block Plan

When starting a plan always place the back block to the left, continue the WL,HL and hem across to the right. Then place the front block on the same WL,HL, hem lines. This will ensure pattern length is correct.

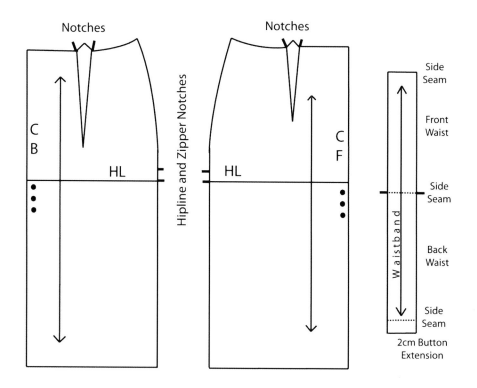

Skirt Block Pattern Construction

To adapt your plan into a pattern you need to add the following:-

1. Add 1cm seam allowance around all edges (NOT CF,CB as these are on the fold)
2. Add 3cm hem allowance
3. Add notches to:-
a. Darts, both top edges
b. Hipline
c. Zipper (18cm down from waistline)
d. Hemline as this is not 1cm
4. Grain Lines on all pattern pieces
5. Pattern information including abbreviations
6. A waist finish – example shows a straight waistband

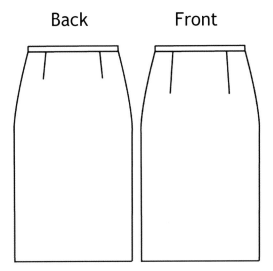

Back   Front

Skirt Block Pattern

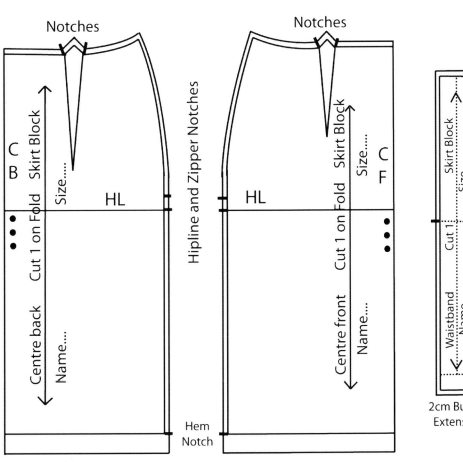

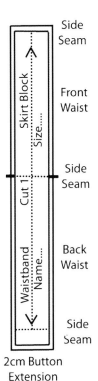

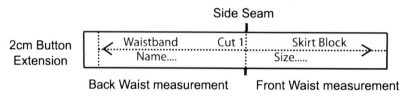

FASHION DESIGN

Waist Finishes

1.   Straight Waistband - when the skirt sits on the actual waistline a straight waistband is used. This is made by measuring the top edge of the skirt pattern and making a straight pattern piece. This can be cut on the fold as it is a straight line. This gives a neat top edge finish with no seam.

Side Seam

2cm Button Extension

| ← | Waistband | Cut 1 | Skirt Block | → |
| | Name.... | | Size..... | |

Back Waist measurement   Front Waist measurement

2.   Low Waist Skirt - Shaped Waistband – lower waist 3cm to 4cm then draw in your waistband height (4cm average). This is a separate panel and is called the waistband. Darts are closed to make one back piece and one front piece. The skirt pattern is made from underneath the waistband. When a low waisted waistband is used it is curved to shape the body – therefore two back and two front pattern pieces must be cut and sewn to have a top edge seam. This waistband cannot be cut on the fold like a straight waistband as you cannot fold a curved edge. The remaining back dart in the skirt needs to be used, however the front remaining dart is now only 3cm in length so can be moved to the side seam and not used.

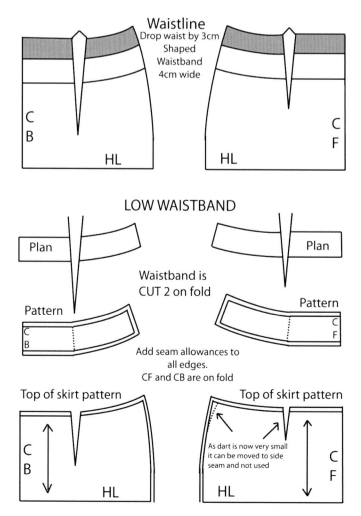

Waistline
Drop waist by 3cm
Shaped Waistband
4cm wide

C B

HL

C F

HL

LOW WAISTBAND

Plan

Plan

Waistband is CUT 2 on fold

Pattern

C B

Pattern

C F

Add seam allowances to all edges.
CF and CB are on fold

Top of skirt pattern

C B

HL

Top of skirt pattern

As dart is now very small it can be moved to side seam and not used

HL

C F

3.   Facing - Sewn onto the inside of the waist - 4cm wide (average). The waist-line has been lowered then the skirt facing is drawn on the plan the same way a low waisted skirt is. The facing is one pattern piece, closing the front and back darts to make one back piece and one front piece. The skirt pattern is up to the top edge. The facing is sewn to the top of the skirt and sits on the inside. This gives a very clean top edge.

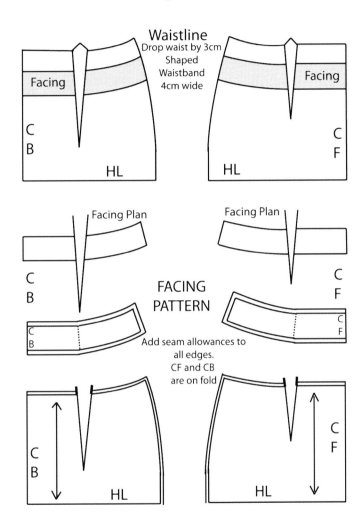

4.   Yoke - A yoke is made in the same way as a low waistband. (No. 2 Shaped Waistband) However when the waistband is wider than 6cm it is called a YOKE instead of a waistband. Close waist darts in the same way as the low waistband. Yokes can be as wide as you design and are used on the front and back of garments. Yokes can be designed into many shapes, with style lines at the top and bottom edge. If the yoke is wide and the remaining skirt darts are very small these can be pivoted (moved) to the side seam and not used.

FASHION DESIGN

Waist Finish Sample Pictures - Front View

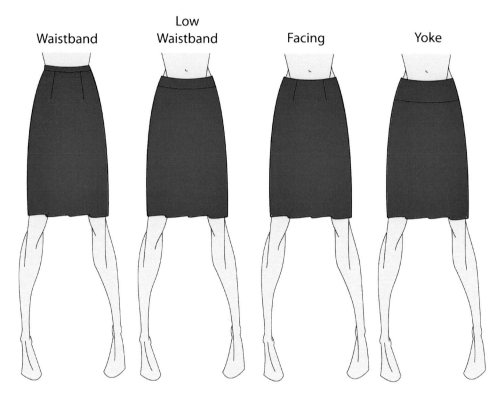

Waistband

Low Waistband

Facing

Yoke

Skirt Yoke Sample Designs - Front View

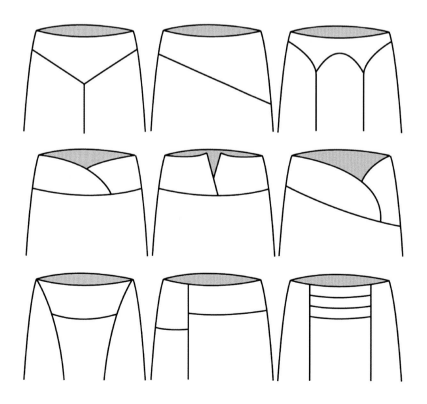

FASHON DESIGN

Pencil Skirts

The skirt block is straight down the leg from the hipline. For pencil skirts the side seam and centre back seam can be reduced from hipline to hemline to make more fitted skirts.

** Do NOT reduce hipline measurement as this is required for body fit. For very fitted pencil skirts a split or vent needs to be added to allow for movement.

Pencil Skirt Plan

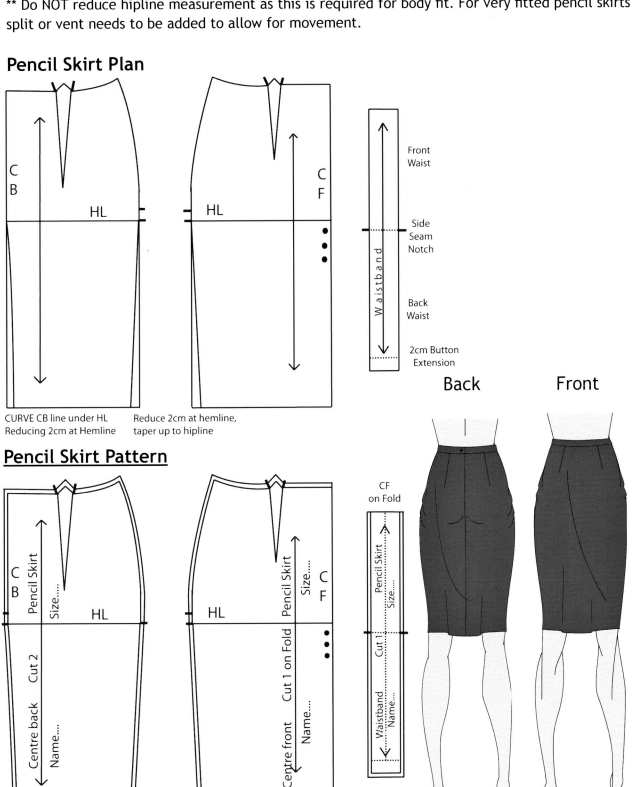

CURVE CB line under HL Reducing 2cm at Hemline

Reduce 2cm at hemline, taper up to hipline

Pencil Skirt Pattern

Back   Front

Full Skirt ("A" Line Skirt)

For full skirt designs the darts can be closed and opened up at the hemline (this is called pivoting) to allow a smoother look at the waist with no darts, and opening the skirt through the middle of the legs. This method gives even fullness throughout the skirt. An additional 2.5cm is added to the side seam to smooth the hipline curve that is on the straight skirt block, and also adds additional fullness at the side to give an all round even fullness within the skirt design.

1. Continue panel line down to hemline.
2. Pivot dart to close – opening skirt at hemline
   ** taking both sides of the dart and placing together,
   moving the side of the skirt out to the side,
   and therefore opening the skirt at the hemline
3. Plus 2.5cm at side seam, from hipline to hem
4. Connect new hemline
5. Same method for front and back

Full Skirt Plan

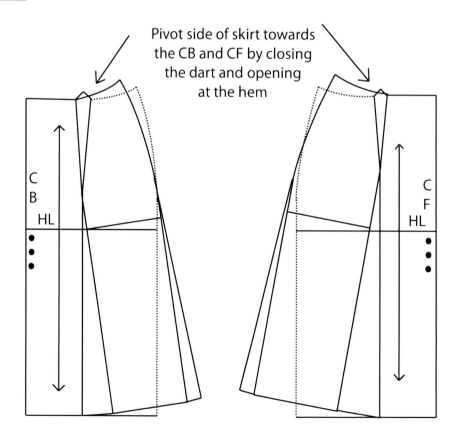

Pivot side of skirt towards the CB and CF by closing the dart and opening at the hem

FASHION DESIGN

Full Skirt Pattern

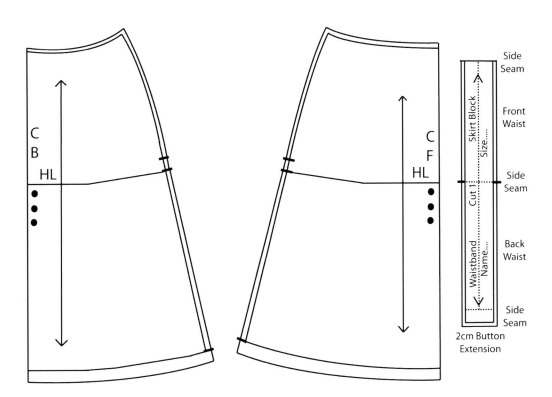

Front View

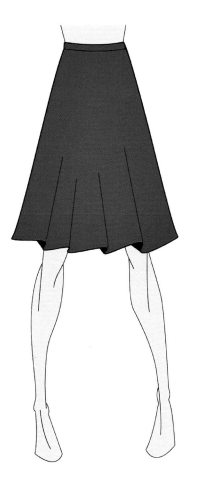

Circle Skirt

For circle skirts a different method is used for construction by measuring the waistline and creating a ¼ circle. The quarter circle is cut two on the fold and therefore creating a full circle.

1.   Copy top part of skirt block. Drop waist by 3cm and mark a low waistband 4cm width
2.   Measure under the waistband
3.   Draw two lines at right angle. Take the waist measurement and draw a ¼ circle
4.   Measure skirt length, front edge and side seam edge – mark this same measurement within the   ¼ circle to ensure hem length is consistent.
5.   Draw in hemline
6.   Circle skirts are cut 2 on fold – front panel being the same as the back.

Circle Skirt Plan

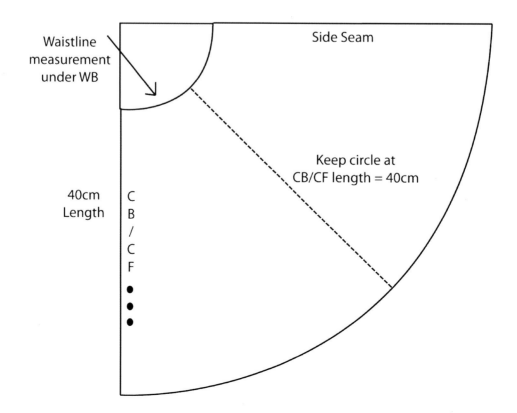

FASHION DESIGN

Circle Skirt Pattern

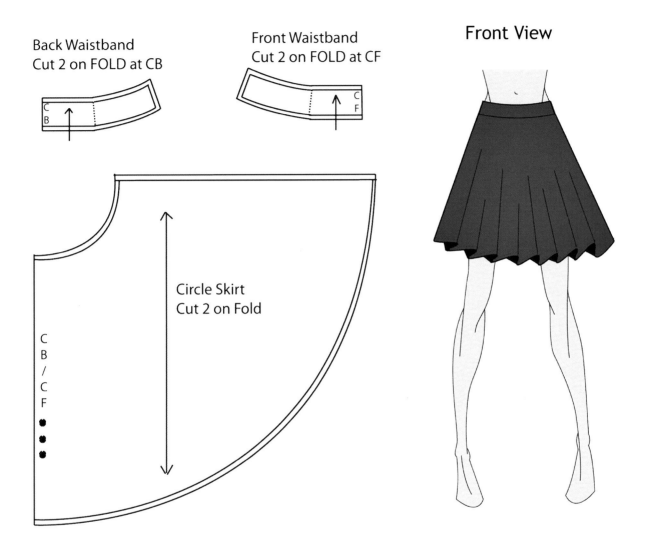

Back Waistband
Cut 2 on FOLD at CB

Front Waistband
Cut 2 on FOLD at CF

Front View

Circle Skirt
Cut 2 on Fold

3. FULLNESS

There are three predominant ways to add fullness to a design.

Pleats can be added anywhere onto any garment. Pleats are generally fixed at one edge and loose at the other to create fullness. If they are placed inside a panel they would fixed both sides. For example a back neck yoke can be pleated but the pleats would be fixed at the shoulder line and back bodice panels.

Gathers create more random fullness. There are two methods of gathering, one side and two side gathers. They can be loose one side, at a hem edge, or fixed into panels by gathering both edges.

Godets are rarely added into a garments body – instead always have the bottom edge of the godet at a hem edge, body hem or sleeve hem.

Pleats

There are four main types of pleats –
Knife pleats
Accordion pleats
Box/inverted box pleats
Sunray pleats

On a plan only the line of the pleat needs to be drawn. The total amount of the pleat must be added into the pattern as when the pleat is closed the pattern is back to the original size. For pleats there are two sides – the part folded under and then the part folded back on itself – both need to be added into the pattern piece to take the block back to its original size. If you wanted a 4cm pleat the total you would need to add into the pattern would therefore be 8cm.

Diagonal sets of lines are drawn on a pattern to denote a pleat, these are the fold lines, for folding under/up and where the pleat sits.

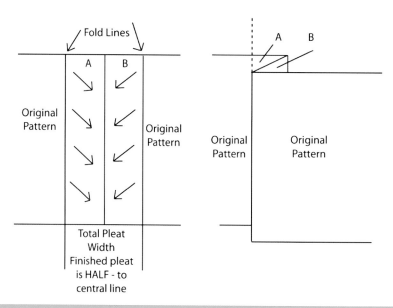

Knife Pleats

Knife pleats are even pleats. Where the amount folded under is the same as the space in which it is being folded into. These give a symmetrical pleating effect. The diagonal lines in the diagram are the pleats. The space in between with no lines is part of your block.

For knife pleats you add the same amount to the folded under and back on itself – so if you want a 2cm knife pleat you add 4cm into the pattern piece. Knife pleats can be any width.

Front View

Knife Pleat Construction

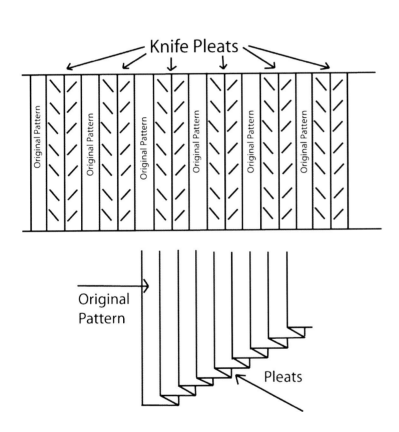

Accordion Pleats

Accordion pleats are the same principle as Knife pleats, by adding in twice the width of the pleat into the pattern piece. The difference between the accordion pleat and the knife pleat is that there is more space between the accordion pleats. This creates less fullness than the knife pleats.

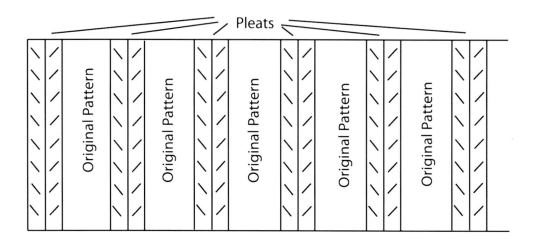

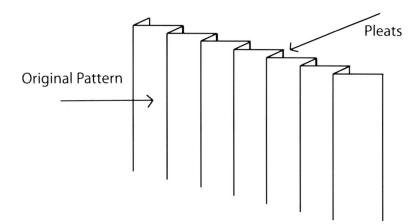

Front View

Box Pleats and Inverted Box Pleats

Box pleats fold out or fold under to the shape of three sides of a box. If the 'sides' are folded inwards this makes an inverted box pleat, where the central part of the pleat is underneath. If the 'sides' are folded outwards this makes a box pleat. Box pleats stand out from the garment.

Construction

The two sides of the box pleat must equal the central part of the pleat. If the side is 4cm, the central part of the pleat is 8cm. Adding in a total of 16cm into the pattern piece.

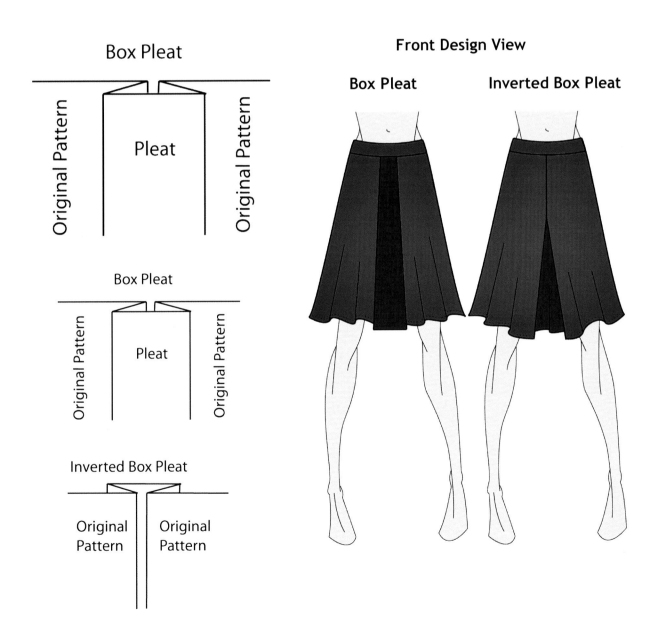

Sunray Pleats

Sunray pleats are smaller at the top edge and larger at the bottom edge. This gives more fullness where the pleat is open (skirt hem, sleeve hem) and less 'bulk' where the pleats are sewn to the rest of the garment. Sunray pleats can be as small as 0.5cm at the fixed edge and as wide as you choose at the hem edge. For each pleat double the measurement needs to be added into the pattern piece. The wider the pleat at the open edge the more fullness you are creating in your design.

The diagonal lines in the diagram are the pleats. The space in between with no lines is part of your skirt block.

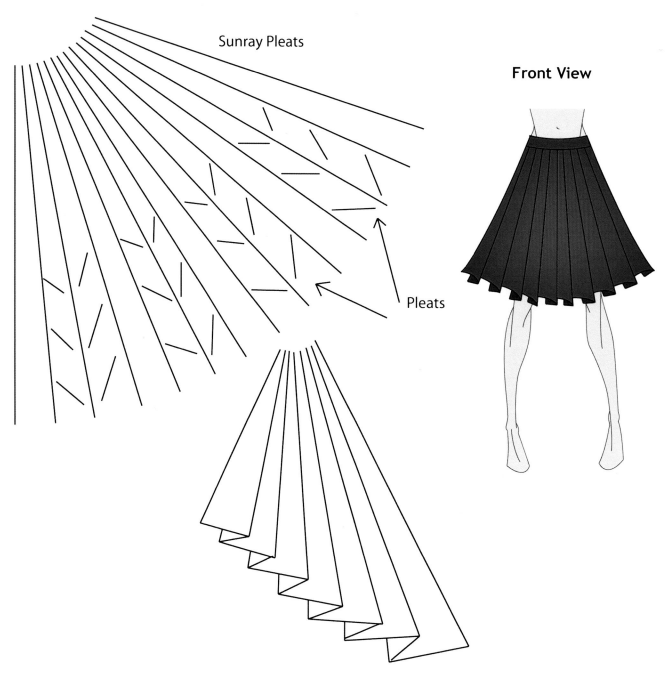

Sunray Pleats

Front View

Pleats

Gathers

There are two main ways to create gathers –

1. Two Side Gathers - When both edges have fullness, one side would be gathered onto a panel and the other creating fullness at the opening. Both sides of the gathers can also be fixed into panels.
Standard gathering is double the original length. For thinner fabrics more than double the length can be used. Two sided gathers plan and pattern is a rectangle in shape.

2. One Side Gathers - When the hem edge only has fullness – i.e. no gathers fixing to another panel but the hem is full. Slash and open one side of the pattern only adding fullness into the hem edge. This creates a circular shape – where one side measures the same as where you will attach it to the garment, and the other side is very full.

** Examples shown uses the low waistband straight skirt (block) separating a rectange 20cm width from the hem of the front and back (joined at side seam). This is then used to create the gathers.

Gathers Plan

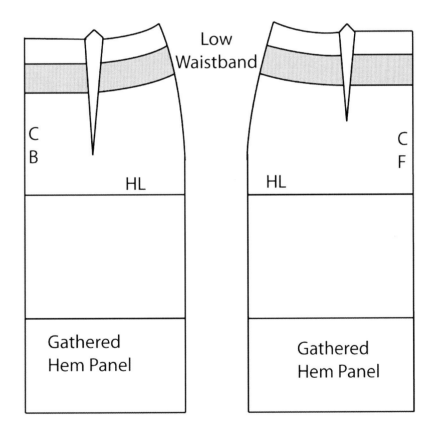

31

FASHION DESIGN

Two Sided Gathers

Two sided Gathers

Original Pattern Piece

Double the length of original piece

Using a gathering thread along the connecting top edge reduce pattern back to original width

Two sided Gathers

One Sided Gathers

One sided Gathers

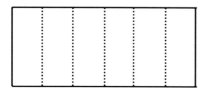

Original Pattern Piece

Mark panels on original for where to add the fullness

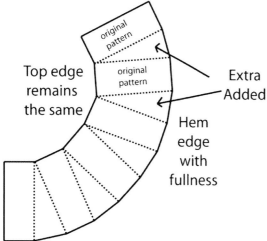

original pattern

original pattern

Top edge remains the same

Extra Added

Hem edge with fullness

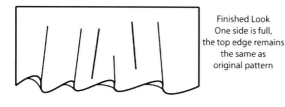

Finished Look
One side is full, the top edge remains the same as original pattern

One sided Gathers

Godets

A godet is a panel of fabric inserted into a garment to create fullness. Used at hemlines and cuffs. The shape of a godet is a triangle – where both of the long sides equal the pattern placement length. The bottom edge of the godet is the width you want to add into your garment.

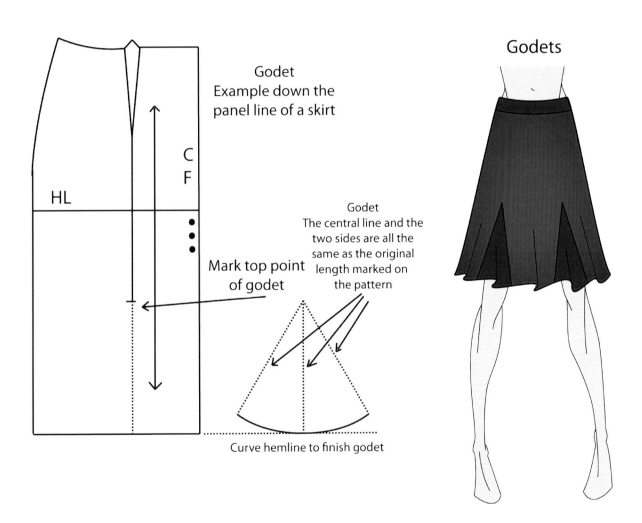

Godet
Example down the
panel line of a skirt

C
F

HL

Mark top point
of godet

Godet
The central line and the
two sides are all the
same as the original
length marked on
the pattern

Curve hemline to finish godet

Godets

4. TROUSER BLOCK

The key measurement required for trousers is the body rise measurement, which gives you the crutch line. This measurement is to ensure the trousers fit perfectly between your legs. Body rise is obtained by sitting on a chair and measuring from natural waistline to the chair. This is the length you need to fit the trousers comfortably between your legs.

Adapting the skirt block into a trouser block - Additional Measurements

Crutch Line (Body rise) = 27cm under WL
Thigh measurement = 50cm
Thigh minus half hip = "X"
Back crutchline = 2/3rds of the measurement "X" + 2cm ease
Front crutch line = 1/3rd of measurement "X" + 2cm ease
CB seam must be raised by an average of 4cm to allow for sitting comfortably

How to Create a Trouser Block

Trousers	Measurement	Size 10
	Trace off the SKIRT BLOCK, keeping HL aligned and space in-between	
0 - 1	HL to CL (body rise) Square across to front leg and mark point 2	7cm
1 - 2 Point 5 Point 13 Point 16	CL to Knee line Square across to back outside leg and mark point 5 Square across to inside front leg and mark point 13 Mark point 16 on the outside front leg	28cm
0 - 3 Point 14 Point 4 Point 15	HL to Hem Square across to front leg and mark point 14 Connect point 5 on the knee line with point 4 on the hem line - BACK Connect point 16 on the knee line with point 15 on the hemline - FRONT	80cm
Point 6 Point 7	Mark a point 1cm in from knee line Mark a point 1cm in from hemline - Join 6 - 7	
Point 9 Point 8	Mark a point 1cm in from knee line Mark a point 1cm in from hemline - Join 8 - 9	
Point 17 Point 18	Mark a point 1cm in from knee line Mark a point 1cm in from hemline - Join 17 - 18	
Point 19 Point 20	Mark a point 1cm in from knee line Mark a point 1cm in from hemline - Join 19 - 20	
Point 10	Mark point 10 on CB HL Slash and add 4cm at HL raising the top back panel. Taper to side leg Smooth CB and side leg lines	
1 - 11	2/3rd of thigh minus half hip + 2cm ease (thigh = 50cm) Join 11 to 6 with a curved line Join 11 to 10 with a curved line	5.4cm
2 - 12	1/3rd thigh minus half hip plus 2cm ease Join 12 - 19 with a curved line Join 12 to HL with a curved line	3.7cm

Trouser Block

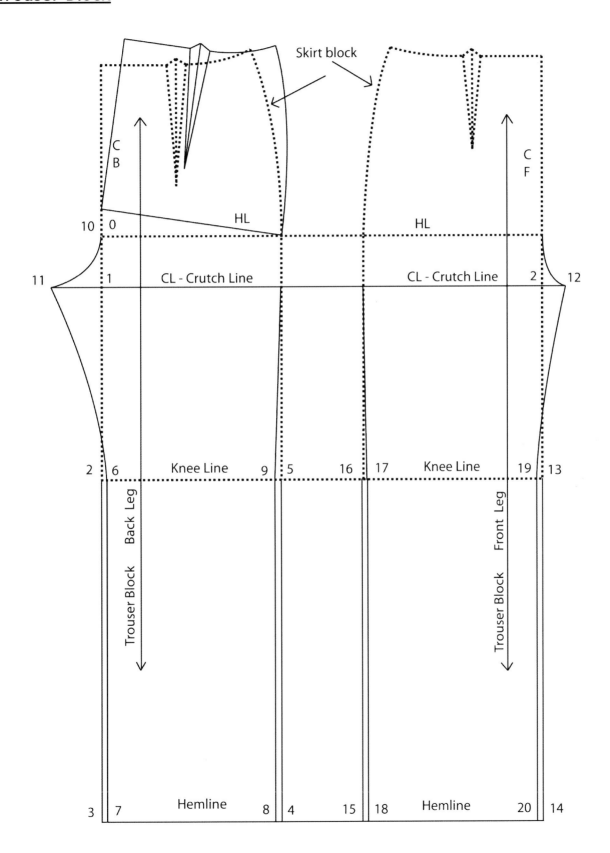

Trouser Block Plan and Pattern with shaped low waistband

The trouser block diagram has been created with a shaped low waistband and a left side zipper. It has a 3cm hand stitched hem. This type of design would be a tailored pair of trousers.

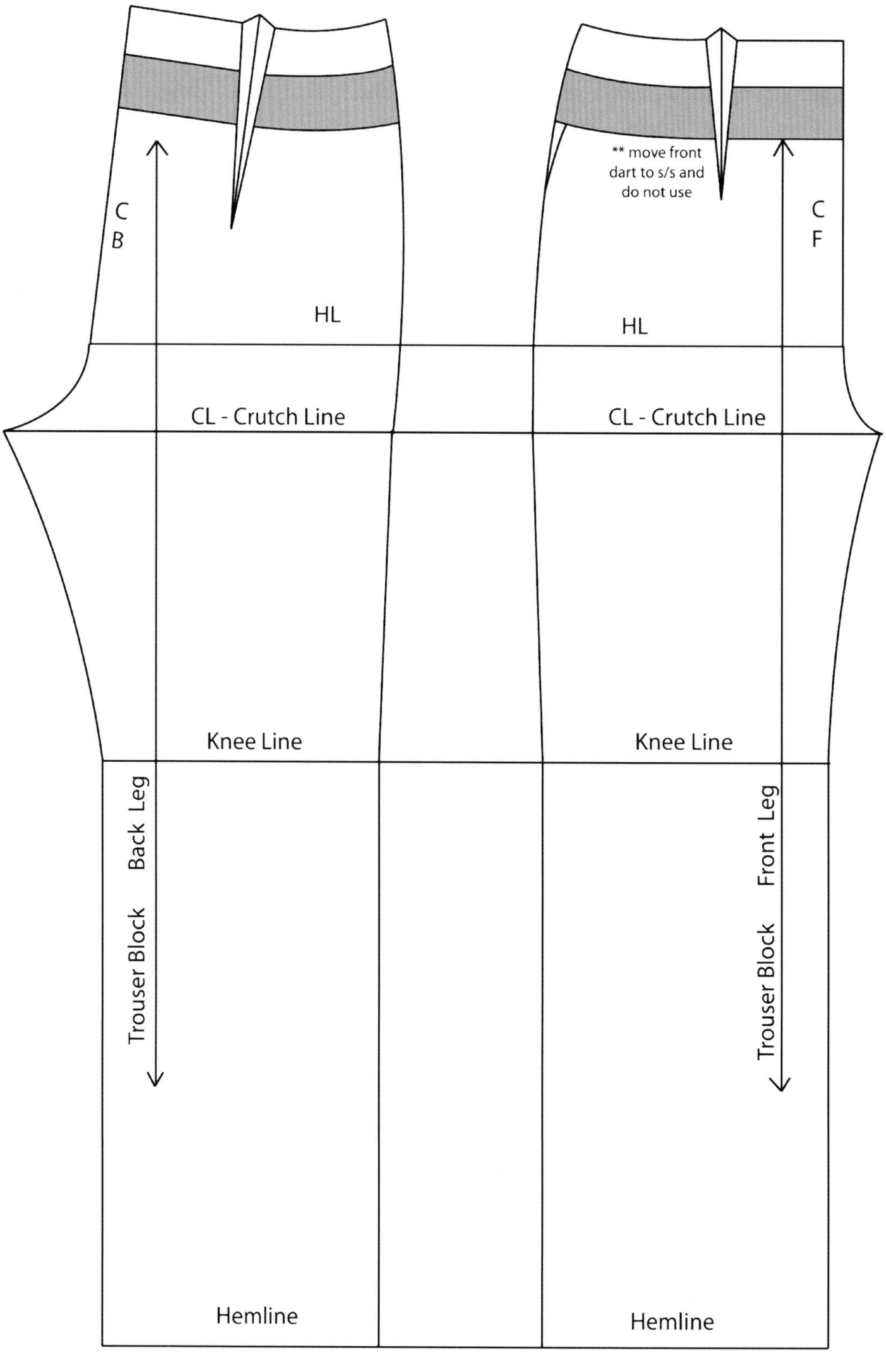

C
B

HL

CL - Crutch Line

Knee Line

Back Leg

Trouser Block

Hemline

** move front dart to s/s and do not use

C
F

HL

CL - Crutch Line

Knee Line

Front Leg

Trouser Block

Hemline

FASHION DESIGN

Trouser Block Pattern

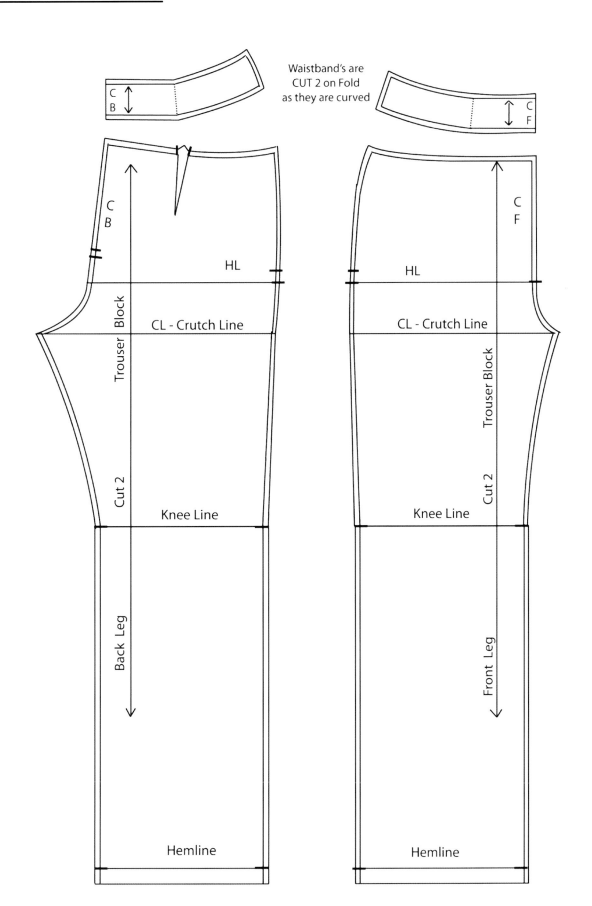

Waistband's are
CUT 2 on Fold
as they are curved

C
B

C
F

C
B

C
F

HL

HL

Trouser Block

Trouser Block

CL - Crutch Line

CL - Crutch Line

Cut 2

Cut 2

Knee Line

Knee Line

Back Leg

Front Leg

Hemline

Hemline

FASHION DESIGN

Trouser Block with Shaped Waistband

Back   Front

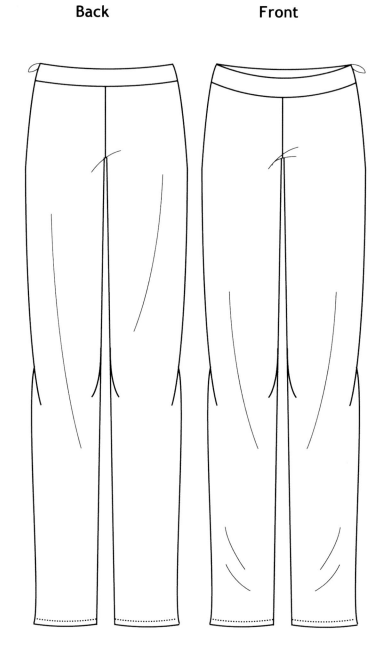

FASHION DESIGN

Fly Front Closure

A fly front is a way of finishing skirts and trousers without seeing the zipper, and having a top-stiched line which curves at the base. It is mainly used in denim jeans and skirts, and other casual clothes.

** For a woman the fly is stitched to the RIGHT. For a man to the LEFT. Women's jeans and casual trousers sometimes have the fly the man's way. A man's pair of trousers never has the fly the woman's way.

Fly Front Plan - Showing Pattern Pieces

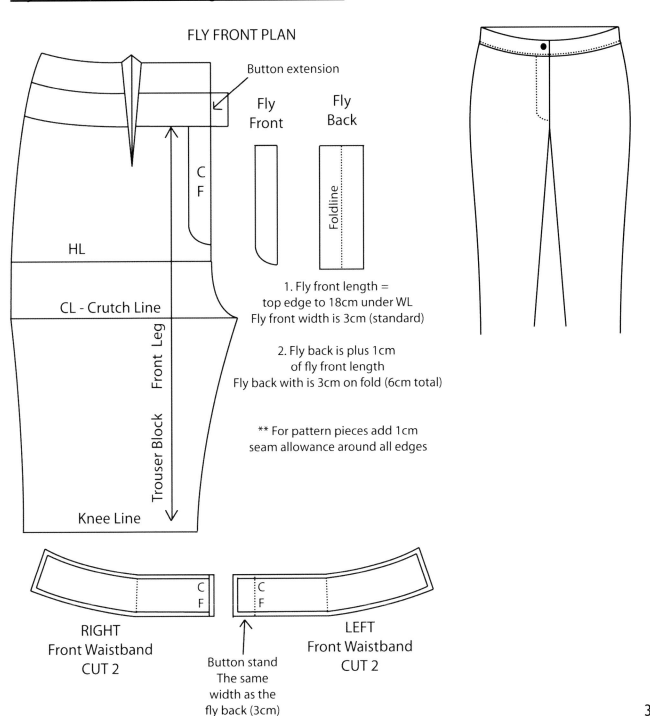

FLY FRONT PLAN

Button extension

Fly Front

Fly Back

Foldline

HL

CL - Crutch Line

Front Leg

Trouser Block

Knee Line

C F

1. Fly front length =
top edge to 18cm under WL
Fly front width is 3cm (standard)

2. Fly back is plus 1cm
of fly front length
Fly back with is 3cm on fold (6cm total)

** For pattern pieces add 1cm
seam allowance around all edges

RIGHT
Front Waistband
CUT 2

LEFT
Front Waistband
CUT 2

Button stand
The same
width as the
fly back (3cm)

C F

C F

Fly front Sewing instructions

1. Sew fly front to outside (right side) of fabric on the right leg side. From top edge to notch.
    Sew one side of the zipper to left leg to notch.
2. Sew centre front seam from notch down to the inside leg seam, stopping 3cm before.
3. Sew other side of zipper to fly front ONLY. NOT to front leg.
4. Sew fly back to left leg side (the side without the fly front)
5. Topstitch fly front to right side front. Women's way.

FLY CLOSURE

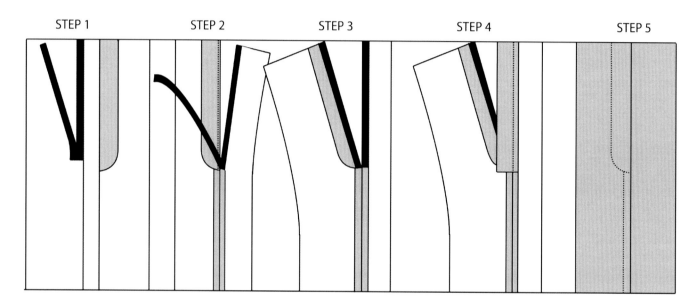

| STEP 1 | STEP 2 | STEP 3 | STEP 4 | STEP 5 |

Skinny Leg Trouser Plan

When trousers are fitted to the leg it is just the leg that is reduced on a trouser block. The hipline needs to remain the same to allow the trousers to fit. On the plan below the hipline ease of movement has been reduced by 2cm only - this will give less movement (ease) at the hipline but will allow the trousers to be more fitted.

Copy off the pattern from the plan in the same way as the trouser block – using the new tighter leg measurement lines.

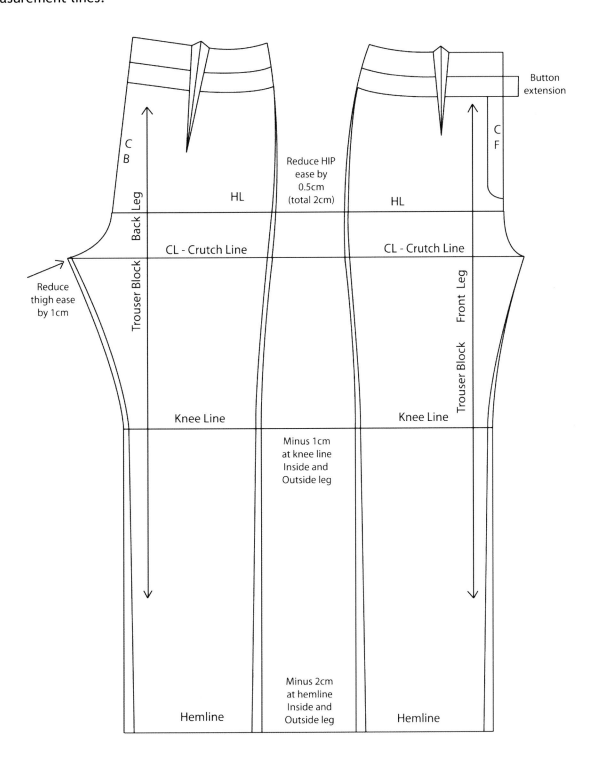

Wide leg Trouser Plan

Copy off the pattern from the plan in the same way as the trouser block – using the new wide leg measurement lines.

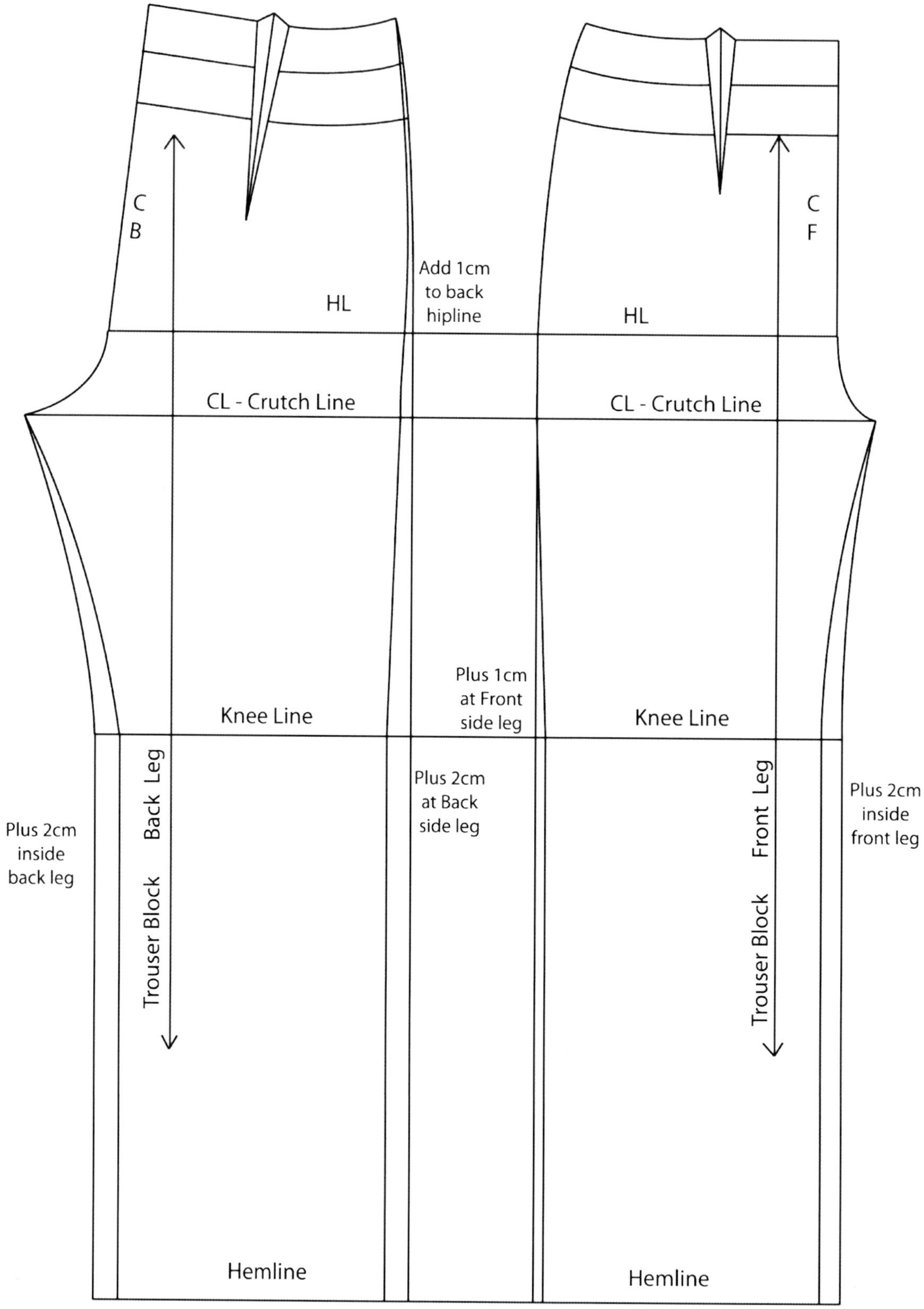

C B

Add 1cm to back hipline

HL

HL

CL – Crutch Line

CL – Crutch Line

C F

Plus 1cm at Front side leg

Knee Line

Knee Line

Plus 2cm at Back side leg

Back Leg

Front Leg

Plus 2cm inside back leg

Plus 2cm inside front leg

Trouser Block

Trouser Block

Hemline

Hemline

FASHION DESIGN

Skinny Leg Trousers and Wide Leg Trousers - Front Pictures

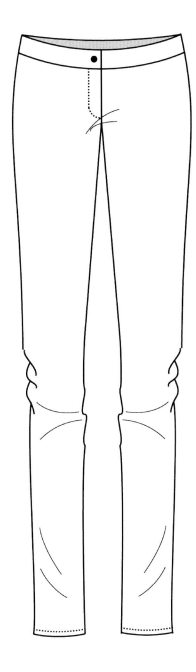
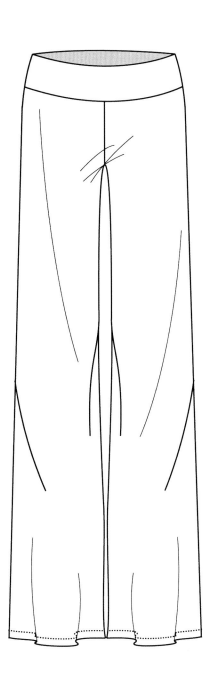

High Waist Trousers

To raise the waistline on trousers or skirts you need to use the bodice block to achieve the high waist shaping – align against the trouser block and smooth the side seams, this makes the waistline slightly bigger but gives a smooth line at the side seam.

Plan

1. Align bodice to trousers and smooth side seam line
2. Draw a line 6cm below WL, front and back
3. Draw a line 8cm UP from WL
4. Add 2.5cm button extension to front waist yoke
5. Draw in fly front
6. Move front waist dart in leg to side seam – smooth line

Pattern

1. Trace off yoke – CB, Side back, Side front, CF panels. The yoke will be on the inside and outside of the trousers for a clean inside finish.
2. CB panel is cut 2 on fold
3. Side back, side front and centre front are CUT 4 – 2 for the inside, 2 for the outside
4. Pattern pieces for fly and fly back
5. Back and front leg patterns – add 3cm hem

The top on this design is now called a YOKE as it is too wide to be called a waistband. The yoke has the panel line seams to give a tight fit and the shaping required to fit against the body.

FASHION DESIGN

High Waist Trouser Plan

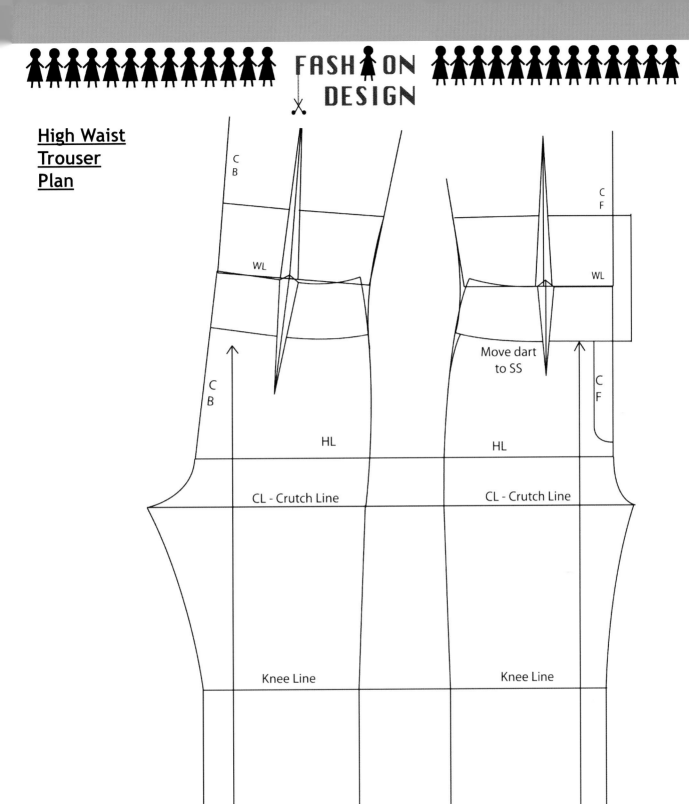

FASH🏃ON DESIGN

High Waist Trouser Pattern

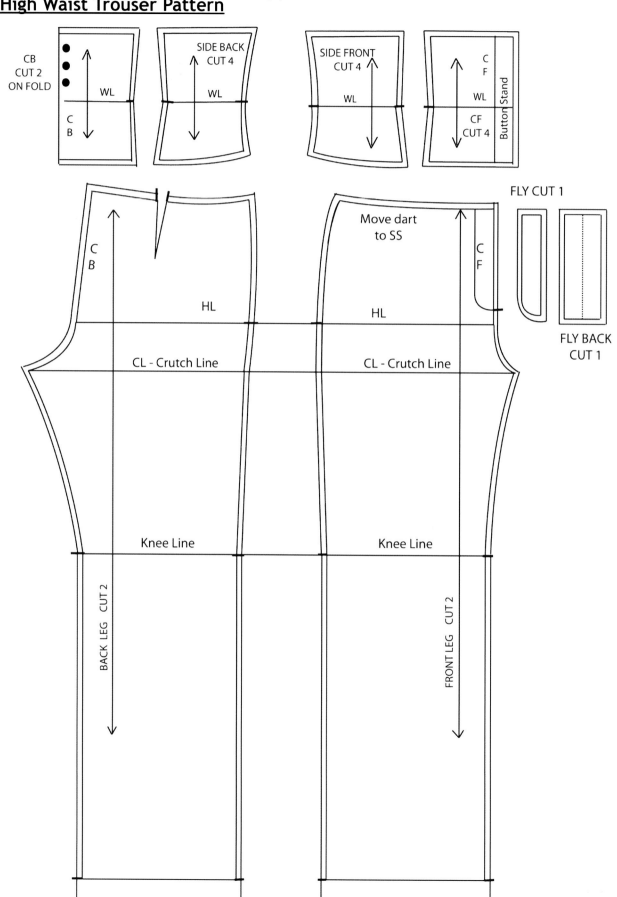

FASHION DESIGN

High Waist Trousers - Back and Front View

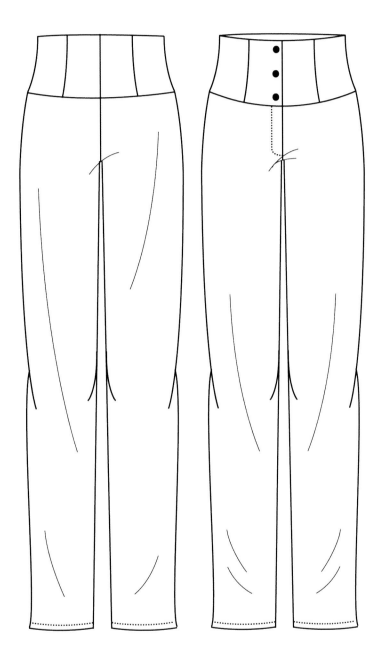

FASHION DESIGN

High Waistband Sample Designs

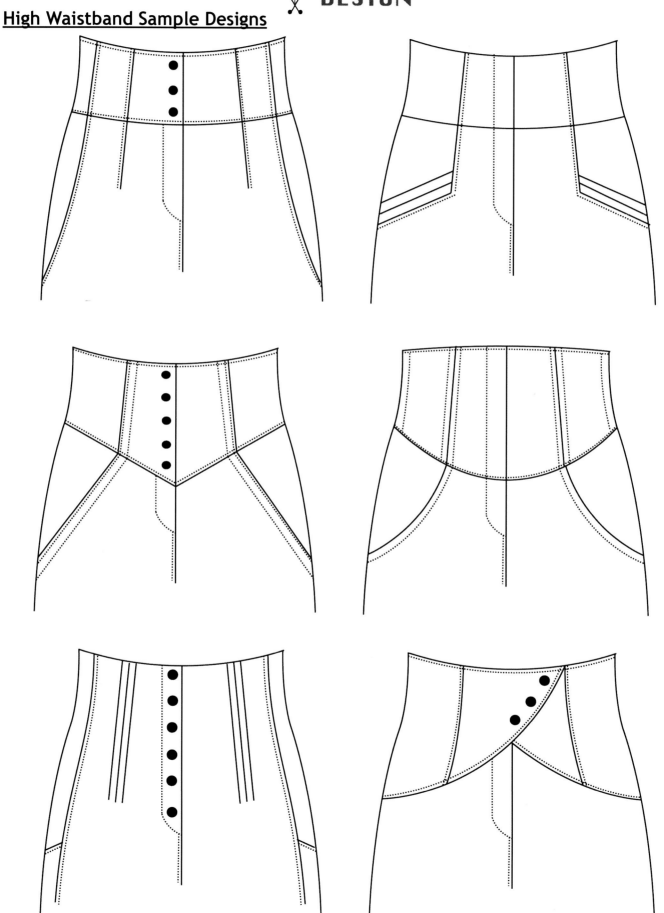

FASH🕴ON DESIGN

Shaped Waistband Sample Designs

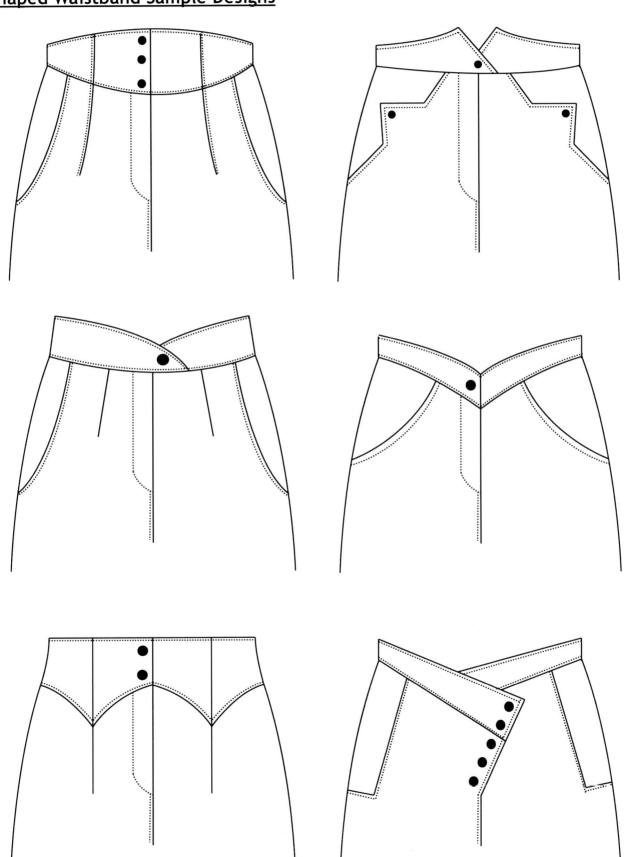

FASH ON
DESIGN

Pleated Waistband Sample Designs

FASHION DESIGN

Belt Loop Sample Designs

Belt loops are commonly used on jeans and casual clothing, but are also used on formal tailored trousers. They can be any shape or design. Common placements are at the side seam, centre back, back dart position and front pocket position.

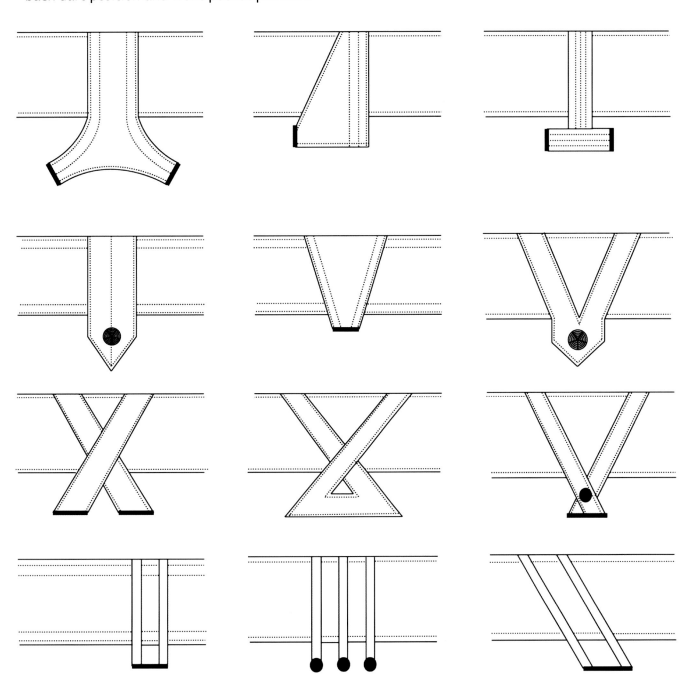

5.BODICE BLOCK

A bodice block is used to make all styles of woven tops and dresses. Combined with the appropriate sleeve block for sleeved styles. The block is constructed to the hipline (HL). For long tops and dresses square down from hipline to desired length on your plan. Refer to measurement size chart for leg lengths.

Many blouses and shirts never end at the actual waistline. A common length is 14cm under the WL. The bodice block is always adapted into designs and very rarely would it be used as it is. Other components would be added to the block to create the design – reshaping the neckline, adding a collar, button stand (opening) etc.

The bust dart can also be moved and manipulated into different positions on the front bodice, although the bust point is always pointing to the same position for the best fit. Darts are necessary to create the 3D form. They can be manipulated and moved to suit the design. The waistline darts can be moved along the waistline position as per design, but their original placement gives a distributed reduction around the waistline, so moving is not encouraged for the best fitting.

The blocks are body measurements with ease added for movement. They are fitted and can be adjusted as per garment design. The ease is 4cm bust, 2cm waist and 4cm at the hipline. Sometimes for more fitted styles less than 4cm ease can be used, but ensure the wearer can move comfortably in the design.

From the basic bodice block you can create a panel line and princess line block. These blocks have the bust dart in different positions which are commonly used in designs of all tops, dresses, jackets and coats. The loose fitting block combined with the loose fitting sleeve block is larger, for more volumous styles. The final block, the camisole, has a reduced bust line ease to allow for strapless and styles with straps where the neckline is open.

Panel Line = a seam from shoulder, through bust to the centre of the waist and down to the hipline.

Princess Line = this block moves the dart into the armhole and therefore creating a curved line from armhole over the bust and down to waistline and hipline.

Loose fitting block = this block does not use any dart. The bust dart is moved into the armhole and not used. This does make the front armhole loose to the body and works best when designed with a sleeve. It can be used for styles without using a fastening to open (putting on over the head) To make even looser styles refer to the outer garment block where additional is added into the side seam and the sleeve is larger.

Camisole block = this block would be used for styles with straps and no shoulder. The ease of movement at the bust line has been reduced for a tighter fit.

Bodice Block Terminology

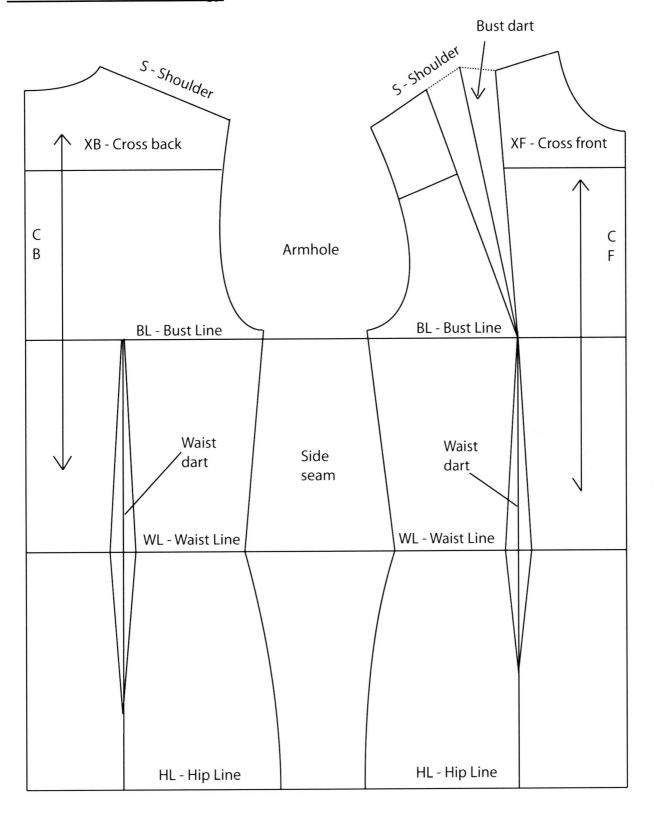

S - Shoulder

Bust dart

S - Shoulder

XB - Cross back

XF - Cross front

Armhole

C B

C F

BL - Bust Line

BL - Bust Line

Waist dart

Side seam

Waist dart

WL - Waist Line

WL - Waist Line

HL - Hip Line

HL - Hip Line

How to Create a Bodice Block

Back

BACK	Measurement	Size 10
0 – 3	CBL Centre Back length to WL Square across from point 0	43cm
0 – 1	Back neck drop	2cm
1 – 2	CB neck point to BL	22cm
3 – 4	WL to HL	20cm
4 – 6 Point 23	HL measurement plus 4cm ease Square UP from point 6 to connect with top line from 0. Mark point 23 at intersect	94cm
4 – 5 Point 9	Half 4 – 6 Square UP from point 5 to connect with top line from 0. Mark point 9 at intersect	47cm
 Point 7 Point 8	Square across from points 2 and 3 to the 6 – 24 line Mark point 7 on WL Mark point 8 on BL	
0 – 10	Half Back neck opening	7cm
1 – 11	(creating shoulder line measurement)	1cm
10 – 12	Shoulder – one side	12cm
3 – 13 Point 14	Back panel line width Square UP from point 13 to BL – mark point 14	9cm
13 – 15	Square down from 13 to HL – mark back waist dart length	14cm
15 – 16	Half back waist dart width	1.5cm
15 – 17	Half back waist dart width	1.5cm
14 – 16	Connect with straight line	
14 – 17	Connect with straight line	
3 – 18	¼ WL measurement PLUS ¼ ease PLUS back dart	20.25cm
2 – 19	¼ BL measurement PLUS ¼ ease	21.75cm
19 – 20	Draw a parallel line to BL UP 1cm – to create base of armhole	
1 – 21	XB position – measured 11cm down from CB neck point	
21 – 22	XB width plus 0.5cm ease Connect 12 – 22 – 20 – back armhole.	17.25cm

FASHION DESIGN

How to Create a Bodice Block

Front

FRONT	Measurement	Size 10
23 – 24	Raise line by 1cm to create neckline and mark point 24	
24 – 25	Same as 0 – 10 (1/2 back neck opening)	7cm
24 – 26	Front neck drop	8cm
7 – 27 Point 28	Front panel line Square UP from point 27 to BL – mark point 28	9cm
27 – 30	Half front waist dart width Connect 30 to 28 on BL	1.5cm
27 – 31	Half front waist dart width Connect 31 to 28 on BL	1.5cm
27 – 29	Square down from 27 to HL – mark front waist dart length	10cm
7 – 32	¼ WL measurement PLUS ¼ ease PLUS front dart	20.25cm
8 – 33	¼ BL measurement PLUS ¼ ease	
25 – 34	Mark point 34 at the line 9 intersect - on line 11 – 12 Connect 25 – 34 with a straight line	
25 – 35	Half one shoulder	6cm
35 – 36	Bust dart width, mark point on 25 – 34 line	6cm
	Connect 35 – 28 with a straight line Connect 36 – 28 with a straight line – same length as 35 – 28	
35 – 37	Half bust dart width Connect to point 28	
34 – 38	1.5cm Connect 25 – 38 with a straight line	
36 – 39	Half one shoulder – point 39 needs to sit on the 25 – 28 line	
24 – 40	XF position – 12cm down from HPS Square line out to dart and mark point 41	12cm
28 – 42	Same measurement as 28 – 41 Square out to the left	
42 – 43	XF plus 0.5cm ease = (40 – 41) + (42 – 43)	17cm
33 – 44	1cm UP	
39 – 44	Front armhole curve – connecting through point 43	

FASHION DESIGN

Bodice Block Construction

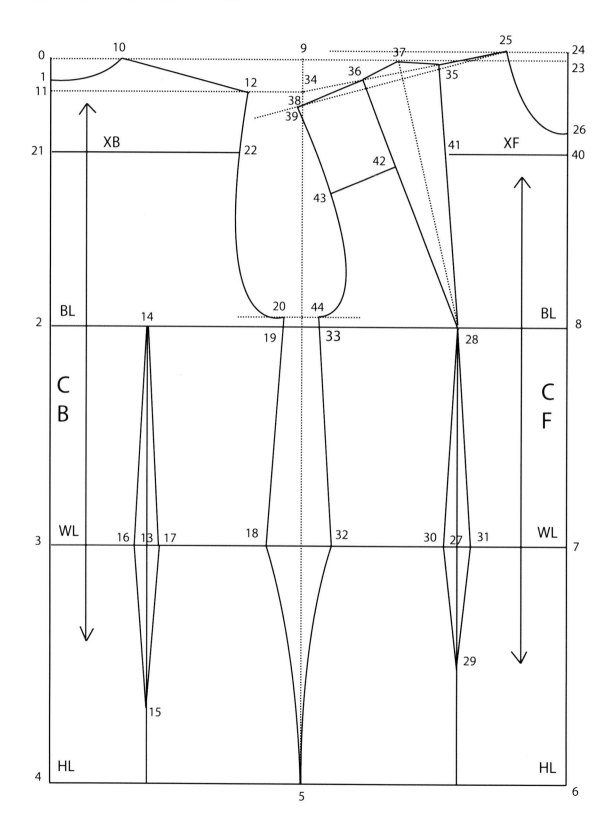

FASHION DESIGN

Bodice Block Picture

The basic bodice block is constructed with the bust dart at the shoulder line - a Panel Line seam.
The picture below shows how the bodice block would look if made into a garment.

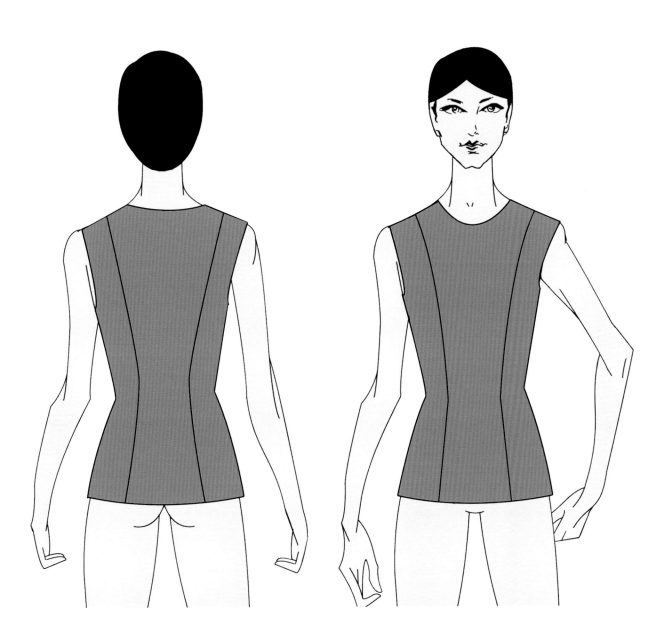

Dart Manipulation

The bust dart can be moved according to the design. See diagram for commonly used dart positions. For fitted garments the bust dart always should be used. The point of the bust dart cannot be moved, only the outside edge. If moved, it will not give the accurate body shaping over the bust.

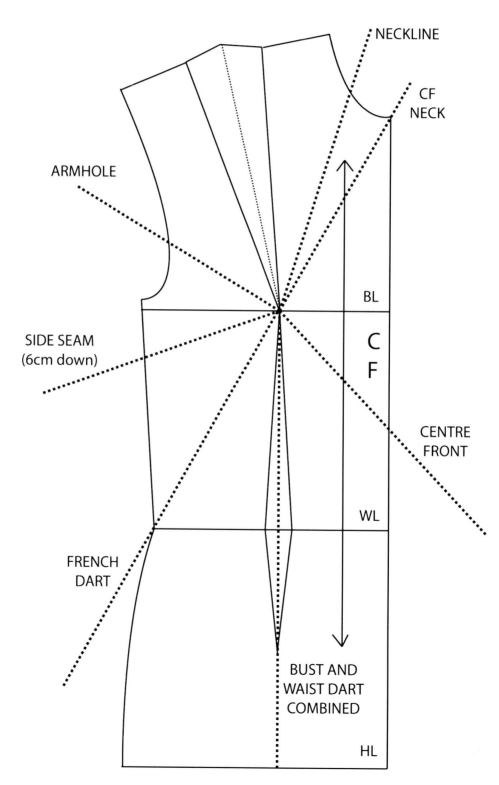

NECKLINE

CF NECK

ARMHOLE

BL

SIDE SEAM
(6cm down)

C F

CENTRE FRONT

WL

FRENCH DART

BUST AND WAIST DART COMBINED

HL

FASHION DESIGN

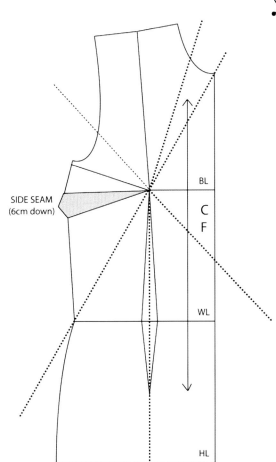

SIDE SEAM
(6cm down)

LEFT
Bust Dart in
Side Seam
Position

RIGHT
Bust Dart in
Armhole
Position

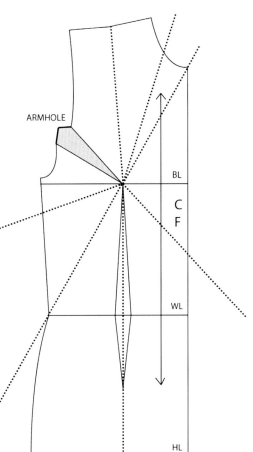

ARMHOLE

**Bust and Waist
Dart
Combined at
Waistline**

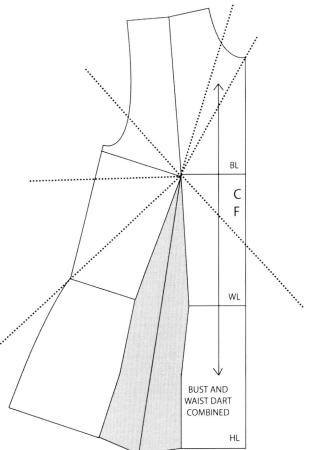

BUST AND
WAIST DART
COMBINED

Panel Line Bodice

Panel lines are commonly used in bodice styles. Where the waist dart continues into the bust dart up to the shoulder line. The back bodice panel line meets the shoulder at the same point.

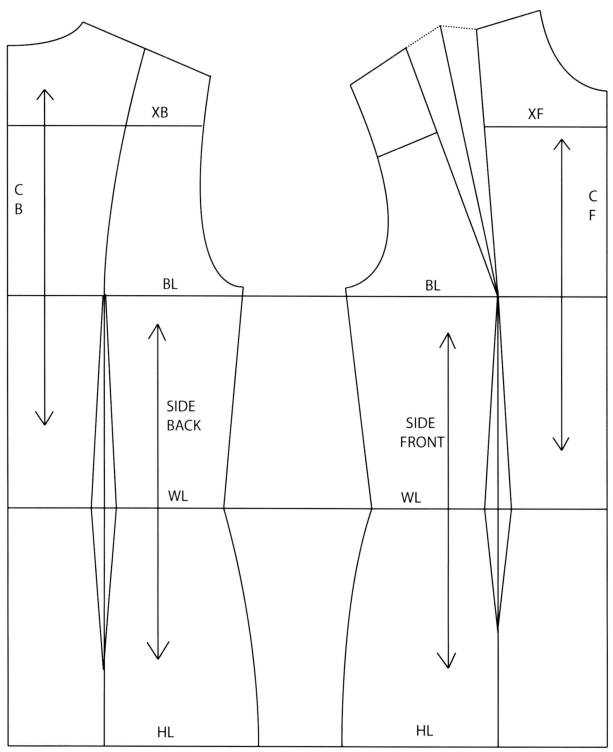

Princess Line Bodice

The princess line take the armhole bust dart and continues down into the waist dart. The bust point is moved back towards the side seam by 1cm to give a smoother line over the bust. The back waistline dart continues into the armhole to mimic the front bodice line, even though there is no dart.

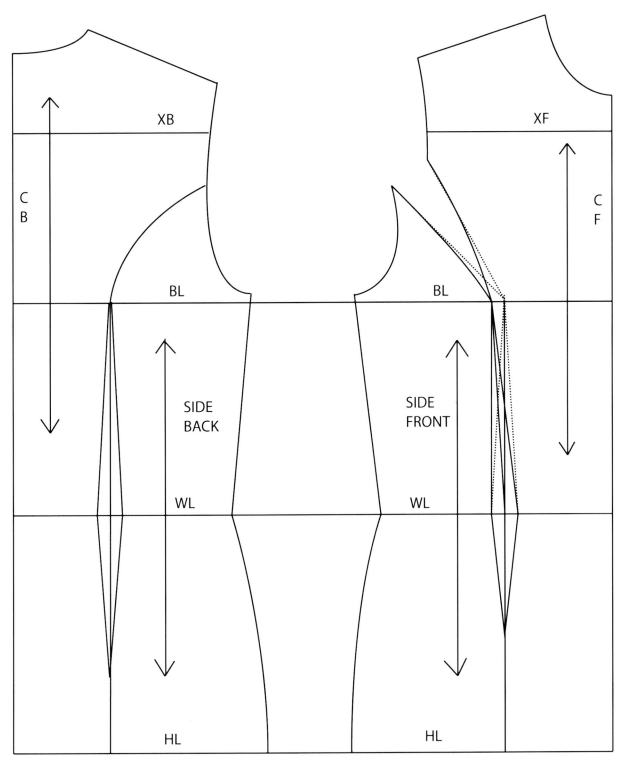

FASHION DESIGN

Loose Fitting Bodice Block

For loose blouses and dress designs the loose fitting bodice block should be used, along with the loose fitting sleeve block.

1.   Move bust dart into armhole
2.   Drop front armhole 2cm. Reshape front armhole – eliminating bust dart in armhole curve
3.   Drop back armhole 2cm and reshape.
4.   Increase WL to BL measurement so that the garment can be made without using a fastener.
5.   Do not use waist darts

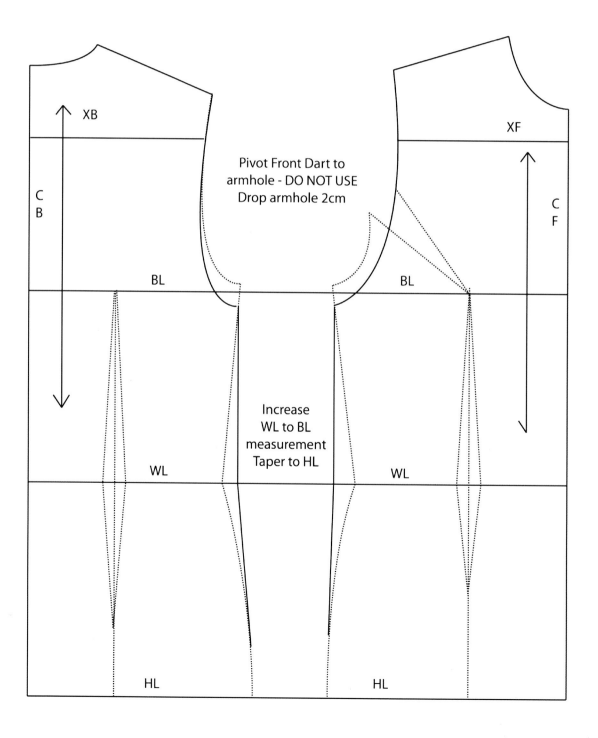

Camisole Bodice Block

A camisole block would be used to make top and dress designs with straps. The bustline has been reduced by 2cm of the ease to make the block more fitted to the body. The armhole has also been reduced to allow for a nicer fit.

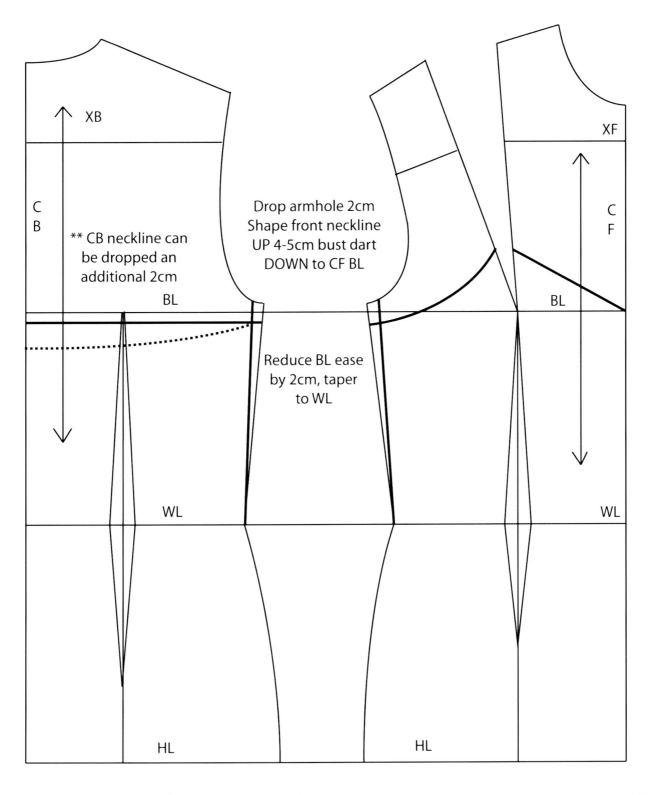

XB

C
B

** CB neckline can be dropped an additional 2cm

BL

WL

HL

Drop armhole 2cm
Shape front neckline
UP 4-5cm bust dart
DOWN to CF BL

Reduce BL ease by 2cm, taper to WL

XF

C
F

BL

WL

HL

FASHON DESIGN

Bodice Blocks - illustrated to 14cm under waistline and not Hip Line, which is a common finish length for tops and blouses.

Panel Line Bodice

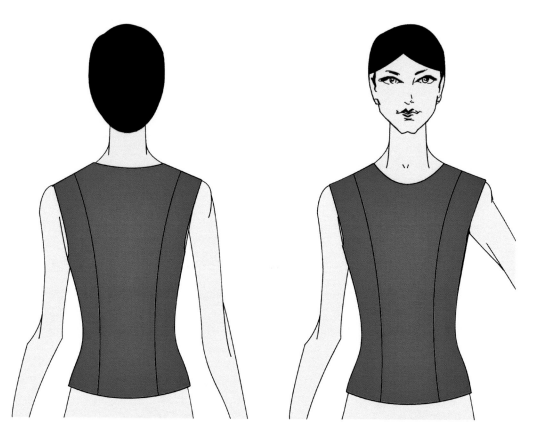

Princess Line Bodice

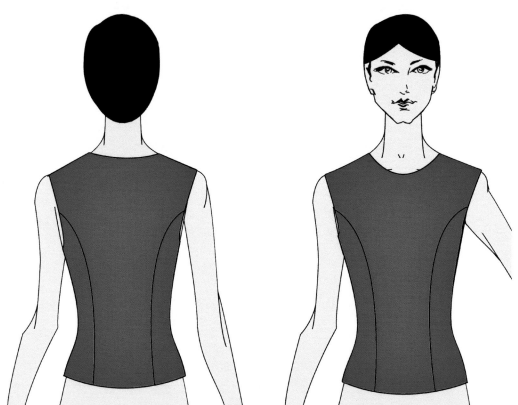

FASHION DESIGN

Loose Fitting Bodice

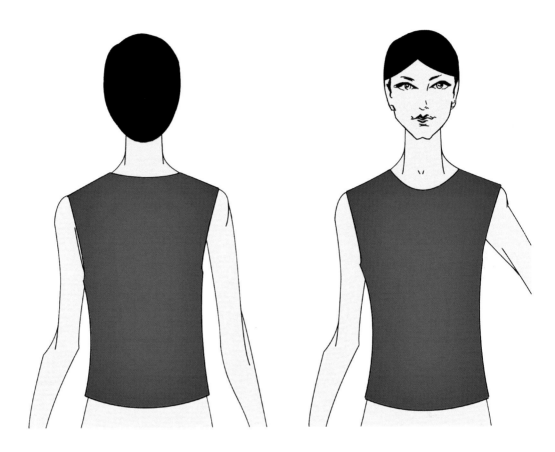

Camisole Bodice

6. SLEEVES

To create a sleeve block you need to know the armhole measurement of the bodice block you want to use to enable the sleeve to fit into the armhole perfectly. The one-piece sleeve block is made to fit the basic bodice block, panel line and princess line blocks. The loose fitting bodice block has a different looser fitting sleeve block.

Sleeve Lengths

Cap sleeve -	10cm
Short sleeve -	15cm - 20cm
Elbow -	35cm
Three quarter sleeve length -	45cm
Long Sleeve -	58cm

One Piece Sleeve - Construction

	Measurement	Size 10
1 - 2	Sleeve Length	58cm
1 - 3	Sleeve head height Draw a line at right angle towards BACK and FRONT	14cm
1 - 4	Back armhole length - draw straight line	23cm
1 - 5	Front armhole length - draw straight line	21cm
1 - 8	Mid point Curve OUTWARDS 1cm midway between 1 and 8 Curve INWARDS 1cm midway between 8 and 5	10.5cm
1 - 7	1/3rd 1 - 4 Curve OUTWARDS 1.5cm at point 7	7.6cm
7 - 6	1/3rd 1 - 4 Curve INWARDS mid way between 6 and 4	7.6cm
3 - 9	Bicep line Square out	2.5cm
1 - 10	Elbow Line Square out	35cm
1 - 11	¾ Sleeve Line Square out	45cm
2 - 12	Half cuff plus 1cm (cuff = 25cm) Connect 12 to 4	13.5cm
2 - 13	Half cuff minus 1cm Connect 13 to 5	11.5cm

FASHION DESIGN

One Piece Sleeve Block Construction

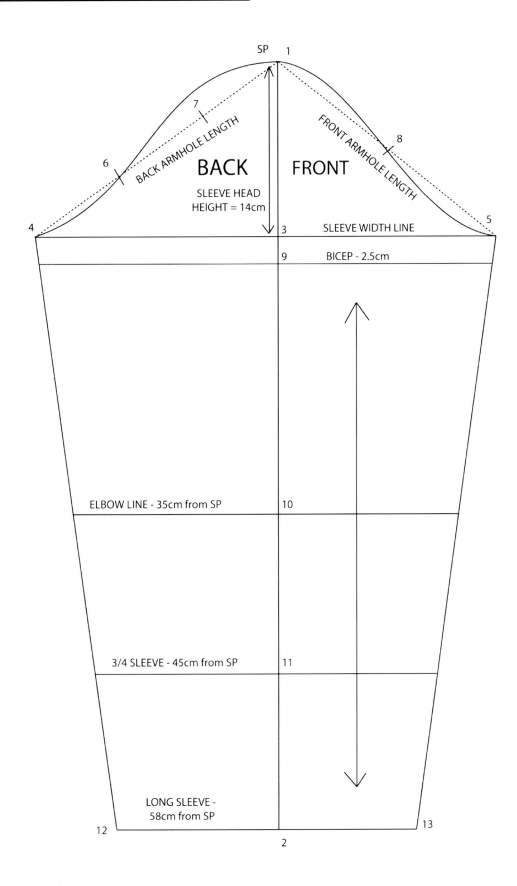

SP   1

7

BACK ARMHOLE LENGTH

FRONT ARMHOLE LENGTH

6

BACK   FRONT

8

SLEEVE HEAD
HEIGHT = 14cm

4   3   SLEEVE WIDTH LINE   5

9   BICEP - 2.5cm

ELBOW LINE - 35cm from SP   10

3/4 SLEEVE - 45cm from SP   11

LONG SLEEVE -
58cm from SP

12   13

2

FASHION DESIGN

Close Fitting Sleeve

The sleeve block has a straight seam from bicep to elbow and hemline. This seam can be shaped for a closer fit but causes a dart on the back elbow.

A second option for a close fitting sleeve is to pivot the dart into the hemline and use a placket or binding to finish the cuff edge.

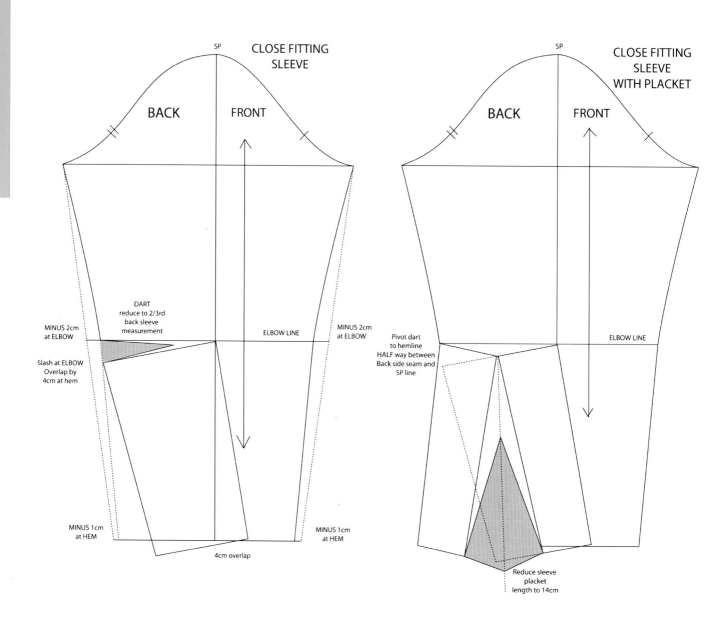

Loose Fitting Sleeve Block

The loose fitting sleeve block should be used with the loose fitting bodice block – where no darts are used within the block. You can create a new loose fitting sleeve block by changing the measurement guide to flow with the loose fitting bodice block measurements. Alternatively you can adapt the basic one piece sleeve block.

1. Extend shoulder width in line with extended bodice measurement – approx 3cm at the Front and Back - take measurement from loose fitting bodice block.
2. Re-align sleeve head line from sleeve width to shoulder point.
3. Add extension down the length of the sleeve front and back by drawing a parallel line to cuff

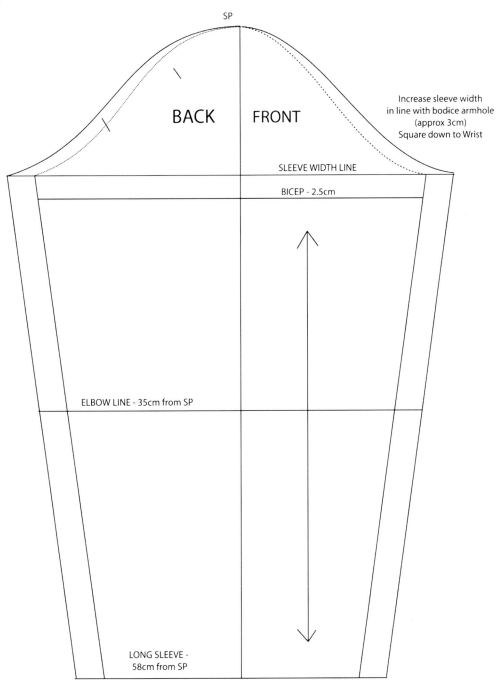

SP

BACK

FRONT

Increase sleeve width in line with bodice armhole (approx 3cm) Square down to Wrist

SLEEVE WIDTH LINE

BICEP - 2.5cm

ELBOW LINE - 35cm from SP

LONG SLEEVE - 58cm from SP

Dropped Shoulder Sleeves

Dropped shoulders can be used in any garment design - from coats, jackets to dresses and blouses. When the shoulder line is extended the armhole shape becomes straighter. Therefore the sleeve head also needs to have less of a curve to fit into the armhole perfectly.

The wider the shoulder = the straighter the armhole = the flatter the sleeve head.

The shoulder extension amount is the same as the sleeve head drop. The side seam extension is the same measurement as the sleeve width extension.

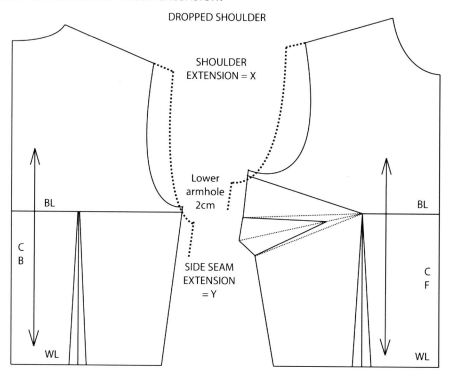

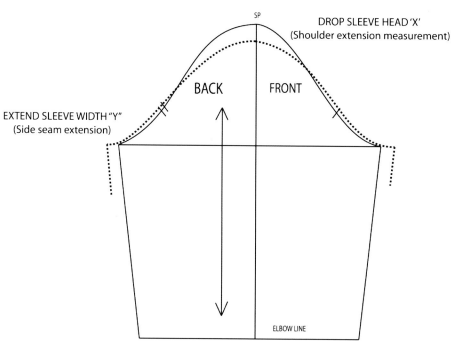

Kimono Sleeve

A kimono sleeve is where the whole sleeve is attached to the body section. Match the shoulder point of the bodice with the shoulder point notch of the sleeve head. Angle the sleeve so that the under sleeve seam touches the side seam of the bodice block. Re-shape the underarm seam to be a slight curve and smooth line. A Kimono sleeve can be very large – amend as per your design.

To create a kimono sleeve you can use any bodice and sleeve block. If you require a loose kimono sleeve design then you can use the loose fitting bodice block and sleeve.

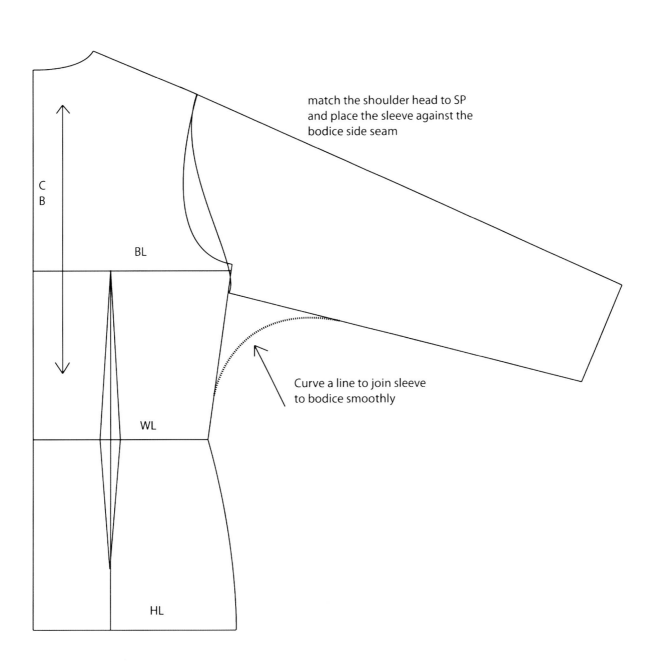

match the shoulder head to SP and place the sleeve against the bodice side seam

Curve a line to join sleeve to bodice smoothly

C B

BL

WL

HL

FASHION DESIGN

Kimono Sleeve Front

For the front kimono bodice the dart can be moved into the armhole and not used. This is good for looser fitting styles.

Where a kimono sleeve is being used for a fitted design it is best to use the bust dart to create better shaping over the bust.

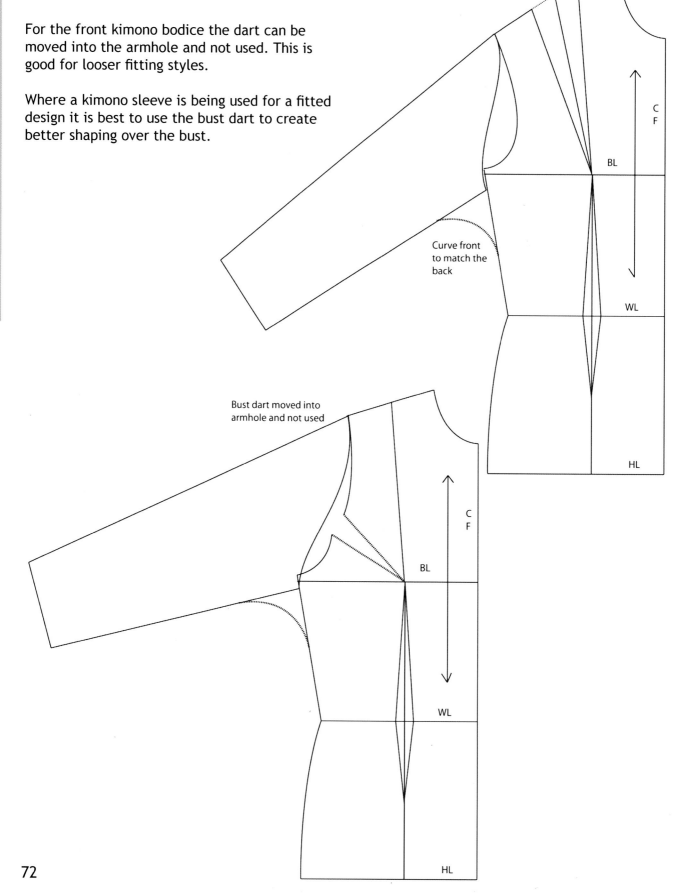

Curve front to match the back

Bust dart moved into armhole and not used

Raglan Sleeve

A raglan sleeve is where part of the bodice has been placed onto the top of the sleeve to create a seam running from the neckline down to the base of the armhole. A raglan seam can be placed anywhere from the CF body to the front shoulder seam, on the back bodice it can be from the CB seam (making a yoke) to the shoulder seam.

What is moved from the front and back bodice panels you attach to the sleeve head, matching at the shoulder point and sleeve head. The bodice part will overlap slightly in places and cause a small gap in other places. Smooth out the new sleeve seam at the base of the new sleeve seam – making sure it is a smooth curved line.

** What is removed from the bodice has to be added to the sleeve with smooth lines. Do not reduce the amount – a little extra is better than not enough.

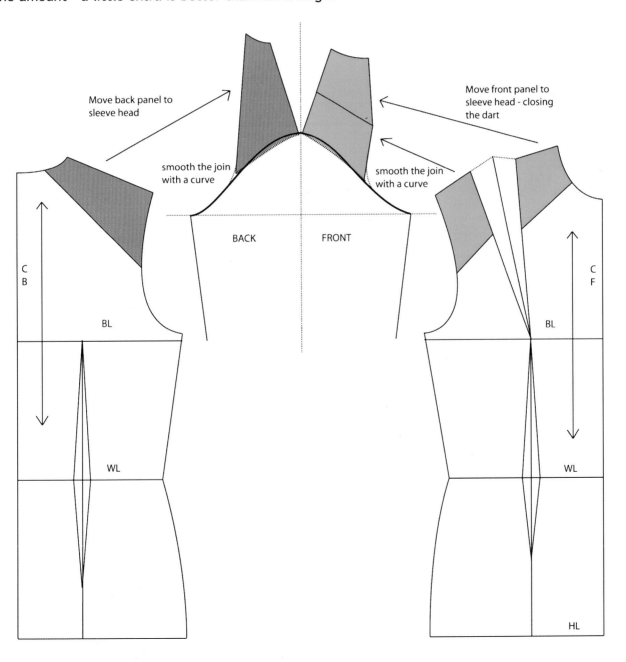

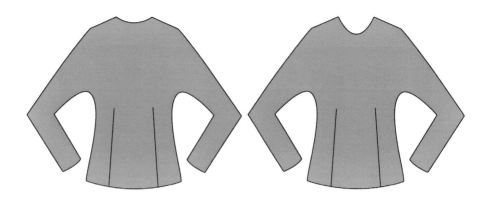

Kimono Sleeve Block Picture

Kimono Sleeve Sample Designs

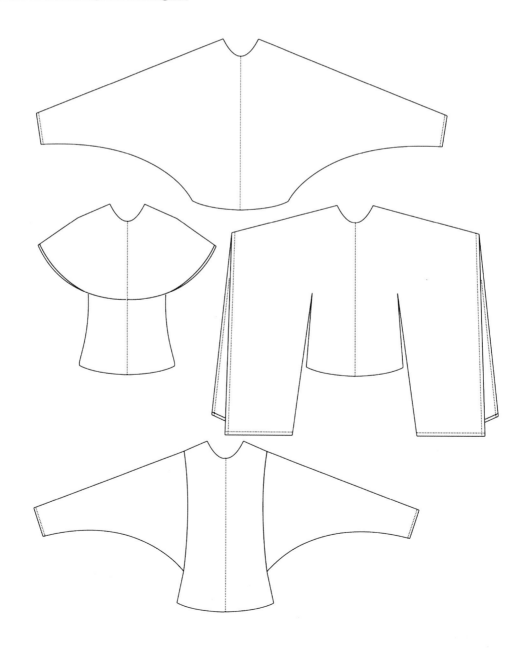

FASHION DESIGN

Raglan Sleeve Block Picture

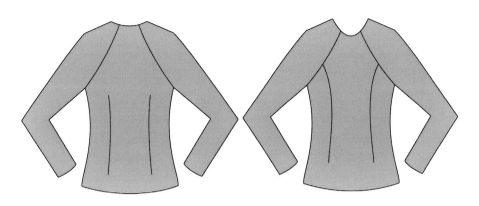

Raglan Sleeve Sample Designs

Gathered Sleeve Head

Using the principle of one sided gathers =

Sleeve

1.   Slash sleeve head into 8 sections from sleeve width line
2.   Add 2cm into each section. Mark new SP mid way between slashed line from sleeve head point (therefore keeping SP in the same position)
3.   Place gathered sleeve head onto sleeve - re-align side of armholes

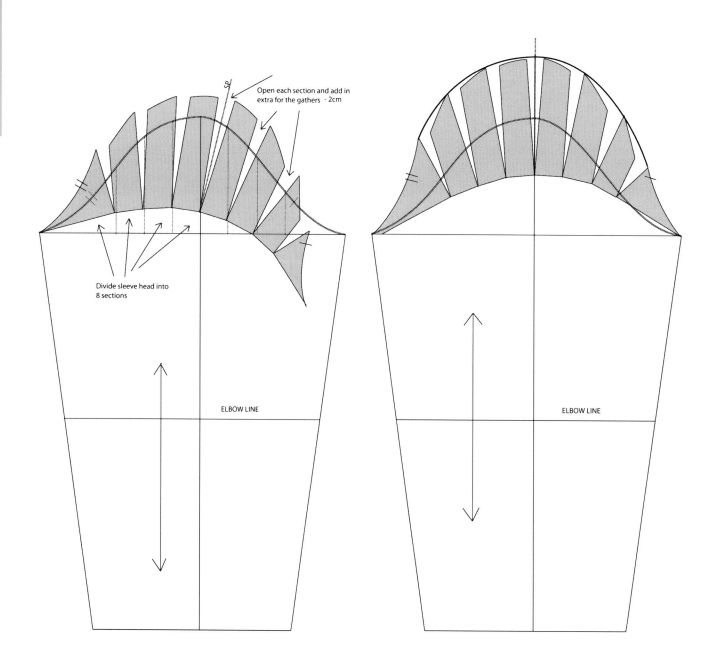

FASHION DESIGN

Bodice

Using the princess line bodice block.

1. Reduce shoulder seam by 2cm at shoulder point, taper to armhole at side seam
2. Neckline shaping - shoulder is 4cm wide, neck drop minus 6cm - connect with a smooth line
3. Sleeve gathers start and stop at notch points so there are no gathers under the arm, just on the top of the sleeve.

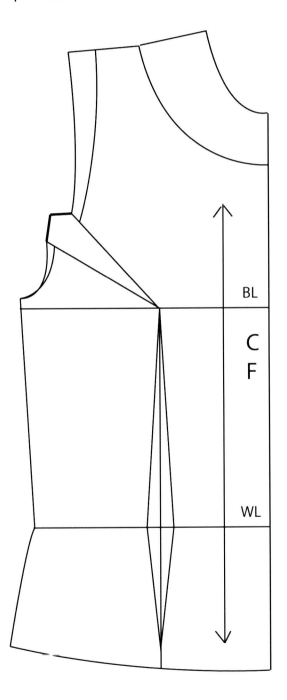

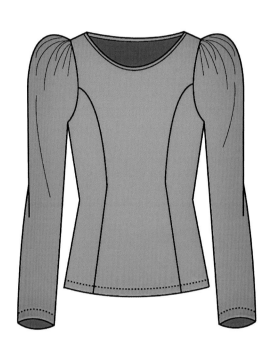

Sleeve Cuffs

To add a cuff to a sleeve hem there needs to be an opening in the sleeve body to allow for the sleeve to be put on, unless the sleeve cuff is large enough to place the hand through it. There are two ways to create an opening in the sleeve.

a.   Sleeve Placket - A sleeve placket is the standard way to finish a sleeve with a cuff. It is made up of two pattern pieces - the top and under plackets. Top placket finished width is an average of 2.5cm. Under placket finished width is 0.5cm. For design detail the top placket can be wider - but the under placket rarely changes as it is just a method to finish the edge and is not visible. Sleeve placket standard length is 14cm but it can be any length, just ensure it is long enough to ger your wrist through the cuff.

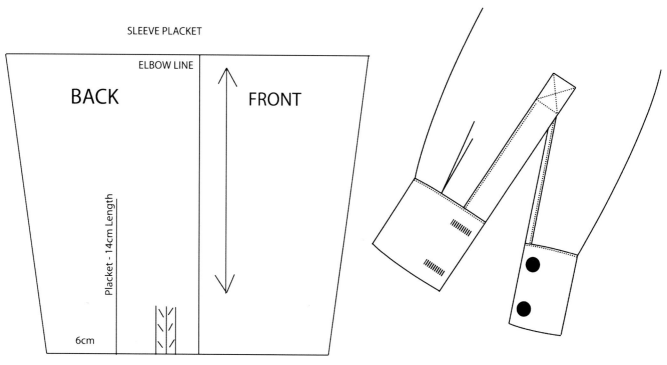

SLEEVE PLACKET

ELBOW LINE

BACK   FRONT

Placket - 14cm Length

6cm

Optional 1cm pleat to reduce cuff size

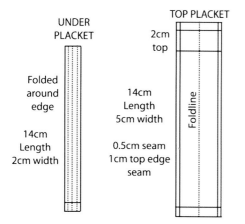

UNDER PLACKET

Folded around edge

14cm Length 2cm width

TOP PLACKET

2cm top

14cm Length 5cm width

0.5cm seam 1cm top edge seam

Foldline

FASHION DESIGN

Sewing a Sleeve Placket

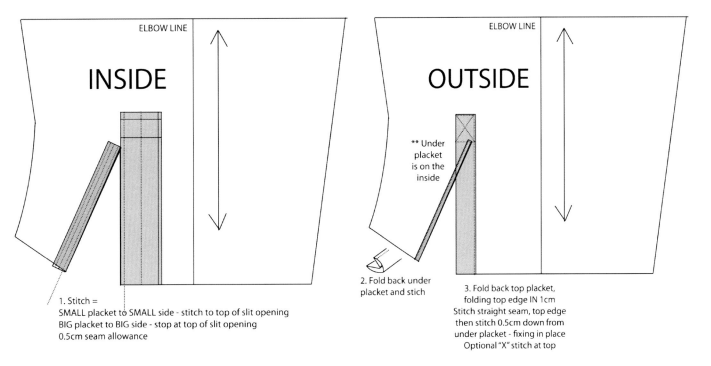

1. Stitch =
SMALL placket to SMALL side - stitch to top of slit opening
BIG placket to BIG side - stop at top of slit opening
0.5cm seam allowance

** Under placket is on the inside

2. Fold back under placket and stich

3. Fold back top placket,
folding top edge IN 1cm
Stitch straight seam, top edge
then stitch 0.5cm down from
under placket - fixing in place
Optional "X" stitch at top

b.   Keyholes – A keyhole finish is generally used on women's blouses and with fine fabrics as it gives a soft discreet finish. A keyhole is made using bias cut binding. The binding is sewn around the slit made in the sleeve and mitered at the top. Keyholes are an average of 10cm in length.

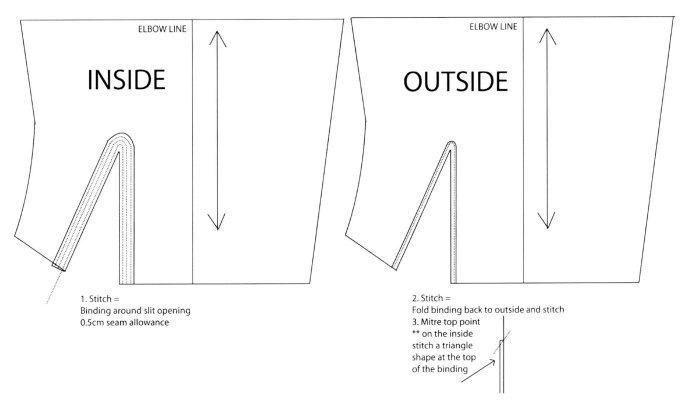

1. Stitch =
Binding around slit opening
0.5cm seam allowance

2. Stitch =
Fold binding back to outside and stitch
3. Mitre top point
** on the inside
stitch a triangle
shape at the top
of the binding

Sleeve Cuffs

A sleeve cuff top edge is attached to the hem of the sleeve. The sleeve pattern can be reduced to accommodate the cuff height or added as extra so that the cuff overlaps onto the hand. The bottom edge, and opening edge of the cuff are style lines and can be any shape or design.

The sleeve can have a pleat or two at the hem to reduce the sleeve hem width and therefore using a smaller cuff width. The cuff cannot be smaller than the size of a wrist with ease of movement.

BASIC CUFF

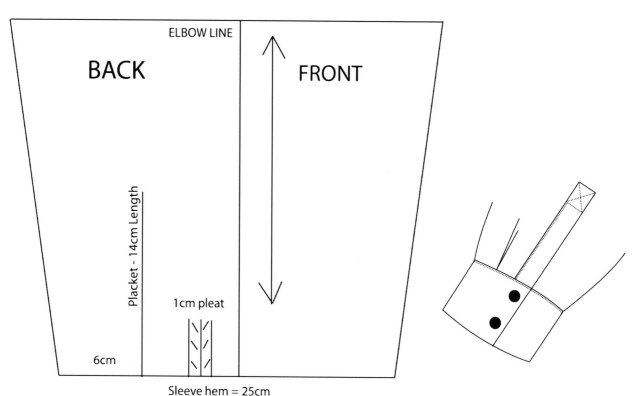

ELBOW LINE

BACK

FRONT

Placket - 14cm Length

1cm pleat

6cm

Sleeve hem = 25cm

Cuff Length = sleeve hem minus pleat = 23cm
** Pleat can be 2cm (minus 4cm)

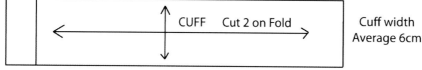

CUFF   Cut 2 on Fold

Cuff width
Average 6cm

Placket
width   ** Sleeve length can be reduced the width of the cuff
Or the cuff can be extra so the sleeve becomes longer

Double Cuff

Double cuffs are worn with cuff links through button holes that's are sewn to the opening edge. A double cuff is double the height plus 1cm of a normal cuff. Folded so that the top (visible) side of the cuff is 1cm wider to allow it to hide the seam joining the cuff to the sleeve. The style line of the double cuff can be any shape or design. The opening edges tend to be pointed, raising 1cm up and 1cm longer, connecting with a point.

A double cuff is still made with a sleeve placket to allow for the sleeve to fit over the hand.

DOUBLE CUFF

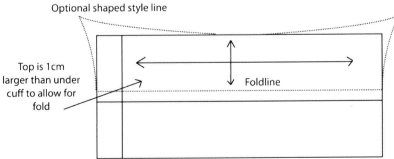

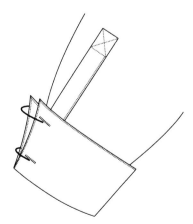

Sleeve Designs

The style lines of a cuff can be any shape or design. The cuff can also be any size – up to the elbow line. The longer a cuff is the more it needs to be shaped to fit tight against the arm.

Basic Cuff Sample Designs

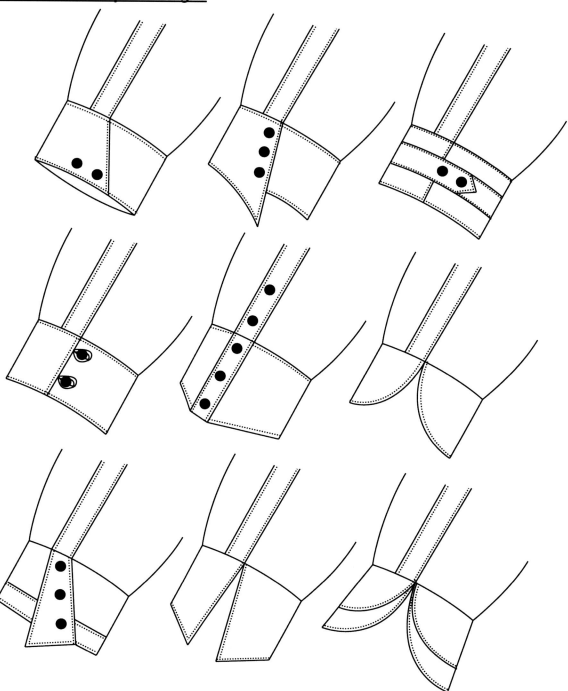

Frill Cuff Sample Designs

Cuffs can be designed with gathers, pleats, even godets. If the cuff is tight to the arm a keyhole binding or placket also needs to be used.

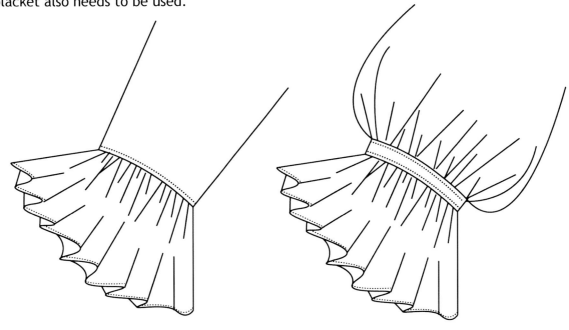

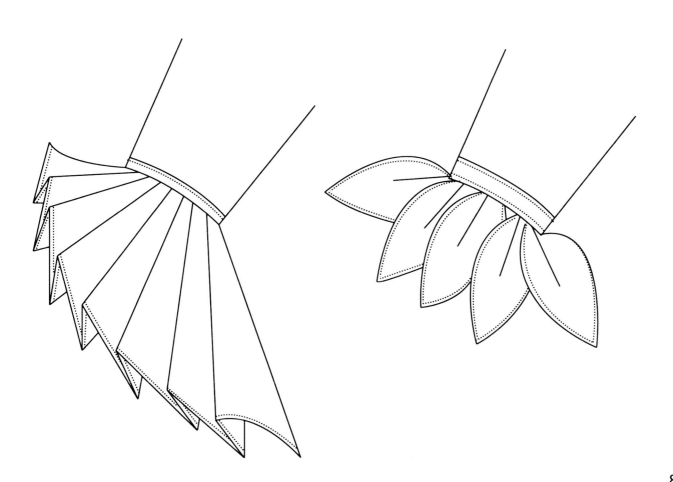

FASH ON DESIGN

Sleeve Hem Finish Sample Designs - With No Cuff

If the sleeve is fitted but you do not want to have a cuff you need to have a keyhole or placket opening to be able to put your wrist through the cuff opening. There are different type of finishes you can design for the cuff.

1. Keyhole binding can be finishing with a binding around the cuff opening
2. Plackets can be constructed without a cuff. Hem allowance needs to be added to double turn the cuff edge.
3. Plackets can also be sewn with a sleeve facing caught inside the cuff.

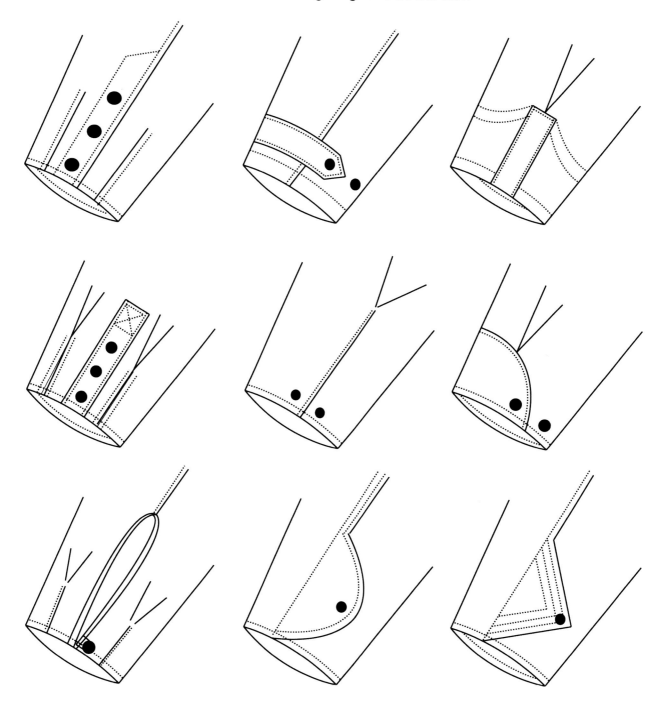

FASHION DESIGN

Sleeve Placket Sample Designs

A sleeve placket can also be designed and does not have to be a rectangular box. It can also have buttons, or concealed buttons to close.

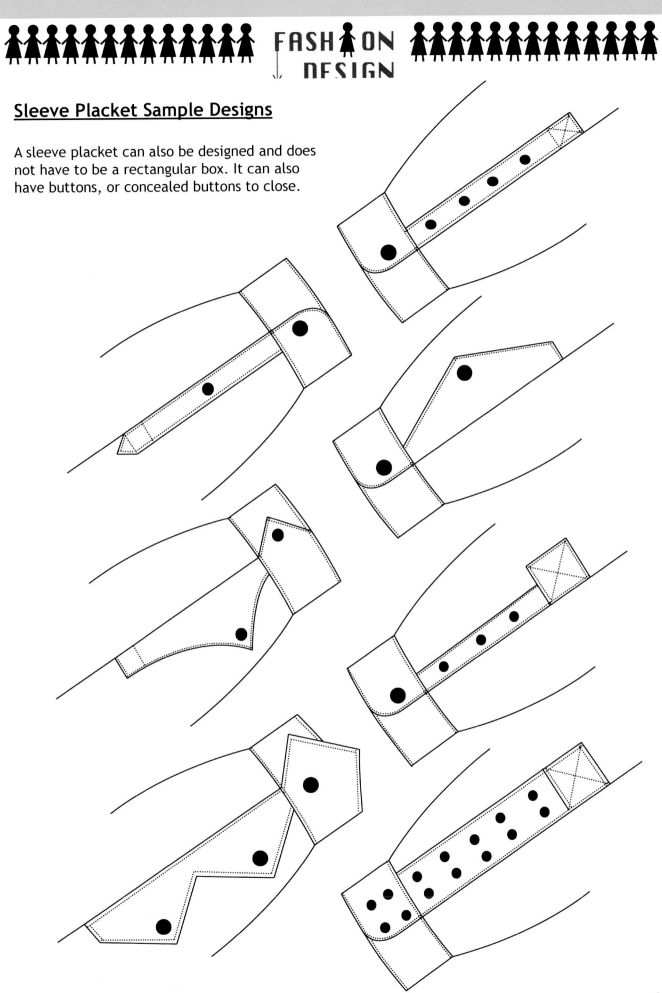

FASHION DESIGN

Full Sleeves Sample Designs - using one side gathers principle

FASHION DESIGN

<u>G</u>athered Sleeves Sample Designs - using two side gathers principle

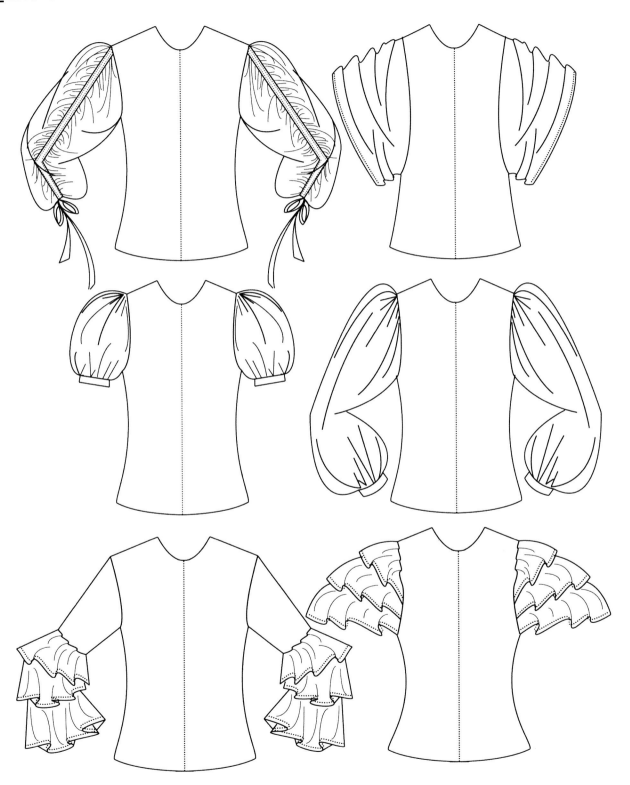

FASHION DESIGN

Pleated Sleeve Sample Designs

FASHION DESIGN

Open Sleeve Sample Designs

7. NECKLINES

When a neckline is not attached to a collar there are two different ways to finish the edge. A facing is predominantly used on heavier fabrics where the neck shape is very fixed. The facing is attached to the top edge of the neckline (with interfacing), then folded to the inside, and is stiched down 1mm in place. Facings can be caught at shoulder seams to secure them in place.

Bindings are used for finer fabrics, and unstable necklines – like a cowl neckline. There are two ways to construct a binding – one is where the binding is seen, and the other is where the binding is on the inside of the neck edge, but a topstitching line is seen on the outside.

When the garment has a lining a facing or binding can also be used. The finishing depends on the fabric and design style. Lining would be attached to the bottom of the facing. For binding the lining would be attached at the top, together with the body onto the binding. Some dresses have body lining but no sleeve lining. The body lining would be caught at the armhole seam and is best finished with binding.

Armholes follow the same principle as necklines – some are better with a facing, and some with binding.

Neckline Finish Construction

Facing

A neck and armhole facing is 3-4cm in width and used with interfacing. If panels have been used in the design close all possible panel lines to create a one piece front and a one piece back facing. Stitch to the neckline on the outside. Fold to the inside and 1mm stitch in place. Over lock the bottom edge of the facing if lining is not being used. Catch by a hand stitch at the shoulder seam.

Binding

Binding is cut on the bias grain and is 2-4cm in width. The finished with is a quarter of the original measurement. 4cm width would make a 1cm binding. Most binding finishes 0.8cm wide. Cutting the original binding piece 3.4cm wide.

1. Visible binding = sew binding to the inside of the neck edge first. Trim and press and fold to the outside. Fold over the raw edge and stitch down on top of the original stitch line. The binding is seen on the outside of the garment.

2. Concealed binding = fold the binding width in half and stitch to the outside of the neck edge. Fold inside, then stitch down to the neckline. This gives a visible stitch line on the outside.

FASHION DESIGN

Facing

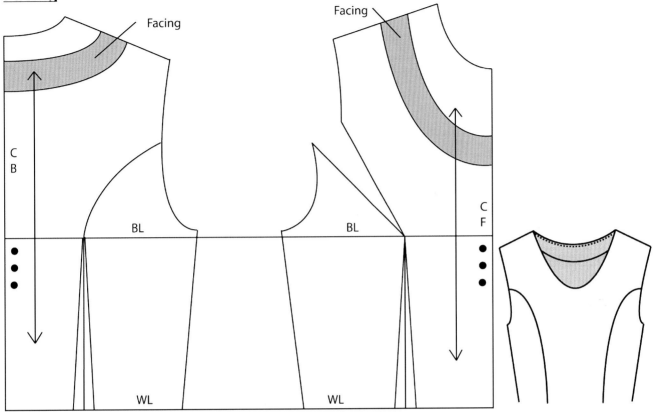

Binding

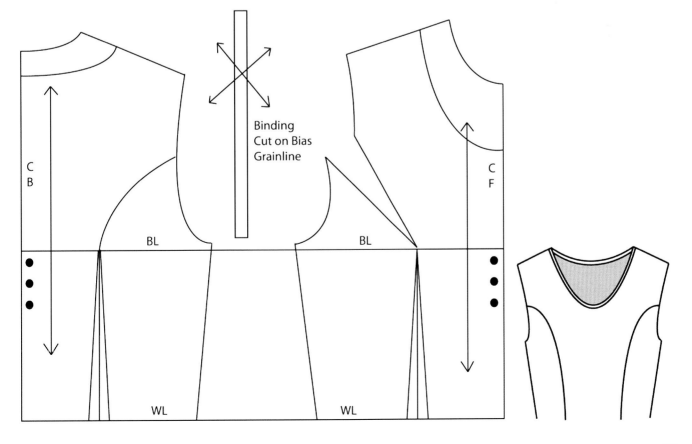

FASHION DESIGN

Neckline Shapes

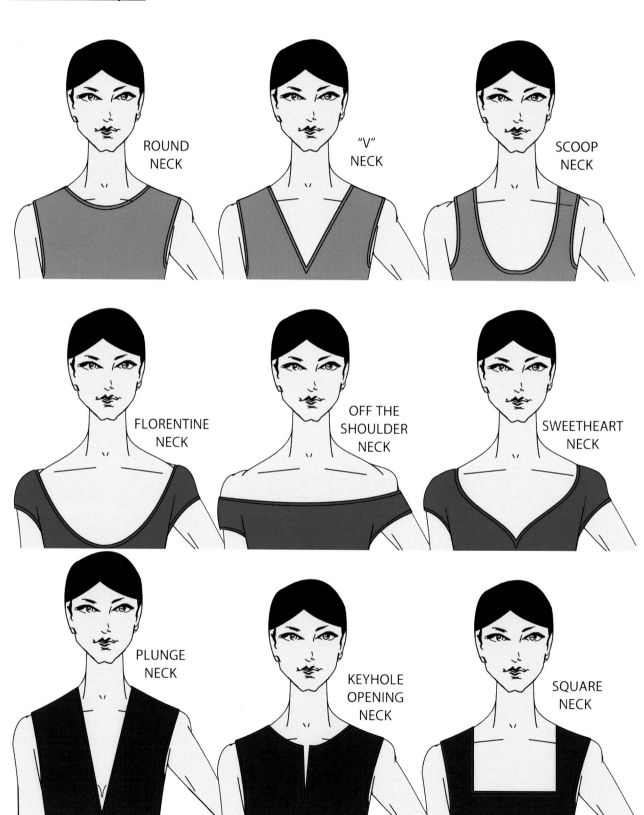

ROUND NECK

"V" NECK

SCOOP NECK

FLORENTINE NECK

OFF THE SHOULDER NECK

SWEETHEART NECK

PLUNGE NECK

KEYHOLE OPENING NECK

SQUARE NECK

FASHION DESIGN

Neckline Shapes

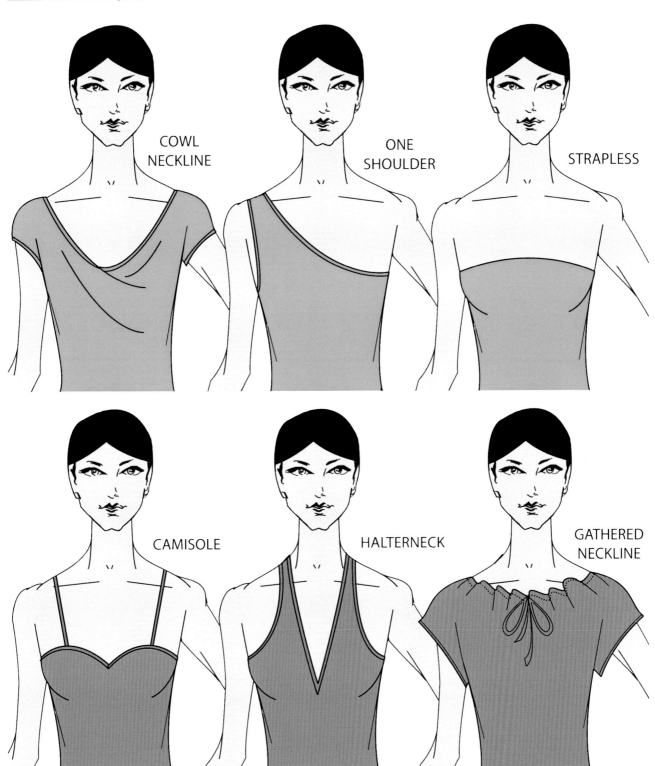

COWL NECKLINE

ONE SHOULDER

STRAPLESS

CAMISOLE

HALTERNECK

GATHERED NECKLINE

93

Neckline Shape Plans

To create some of the neckline shapes you need to adjust the front and back neck shape from the bodice block. When you widen the front neck you must also widen the back neck the same amount so that the shoulder seam matches. The back neck drop can also be adjusted for a lower back neckline. The following designs just require adapting the neckline and shoulder seam to the finished design.

Round Neck, Scoop Neck, Florentine Neck. Sweetheart Neck, Plunge Neck, "V" Neck, Square Neck, One Shoulder Neckline, Strapless and Camisoles.

Off Shoulder Neckline Plan

To create an off shoulder design the sleeve head needs to be reduced the same amount that was taken away from the armhole seam on the front and back bodice. The neckline needs to be finished with either binding or facing, depending on the thickness and stability of the fabric.

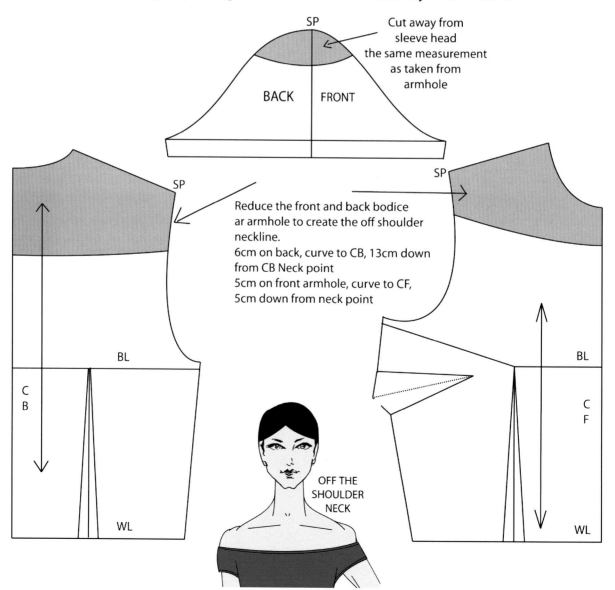

SP

Cut away from sleeve head the same measurement as taken from armhole

BACK   FRONT

SP

SP

Reduce the front and back bodice ar armhole to create the off shoulder neckline.
6cm on back, curve to CB, 13cm down from CB Neck point
5cm on front armhole, curve to CF, 5cm down from neck point

BL

BL

C
B

C
F

WL

OFF THE
SHOULDER
NECK

WL

FASH ON DESIGN

Halter Neck Plan

A halter neck is made where the front bodice is extended at the neckline into a strap that ties or fixes at the back neckline. The bodice at the back has no top back coverage.

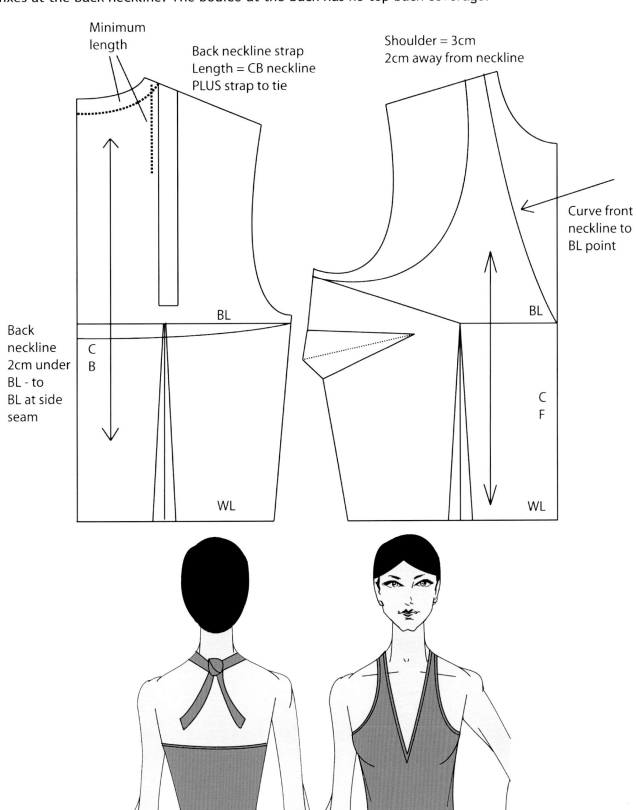

Minimum length

Back neckline strap
Length = CB neckline
PLUS strap to tie

Shoulder = 3cm
2cm away from neckline

Curve front neckline to BL point

Back neckline 2cm under BL - to BL at side seam

BL

C B

BL

C F

WL

WL

Cowl Neckline Plan

A Cowl is where a pattern piece is extended to cause draping. A front neckline cowl works best in soft fabric to allow the fabric to drape into folds down the front. The back neckline does not change to ensure the garment stays on the shoulder.

Cowl back necklines also look good on eveningwear particularly. However do not drape both front and back neckline unless you have straps to ensure the garment stays on the shoulder and does not fall off. The neckline is best finished with binding as the inside of the fabric will also be seen on the finished garment.

Back Bodice
CB neckline - Reduce shoulder by 6cm, curve to CB, dropping CB neckline by 5cm.

Front Bodice
Move the bust dart into the neckline.
Extend the CF line outwards at neckline by 6cm. Taper to WL.
More can be added but then the bust will be revealed.
Mark point on shoulder line at 6cm from neckpoint. Create new neckline by joining the shoulder to the CF edge, ending in a right angle at top CF.

For a grown on dropped shoulder extend the shoulder line by 4cm
Drop the armhole by 1cm
Reshape new armhole

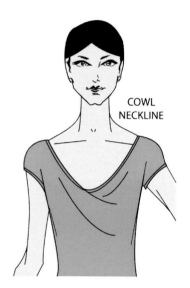

COWL
NECKLINE

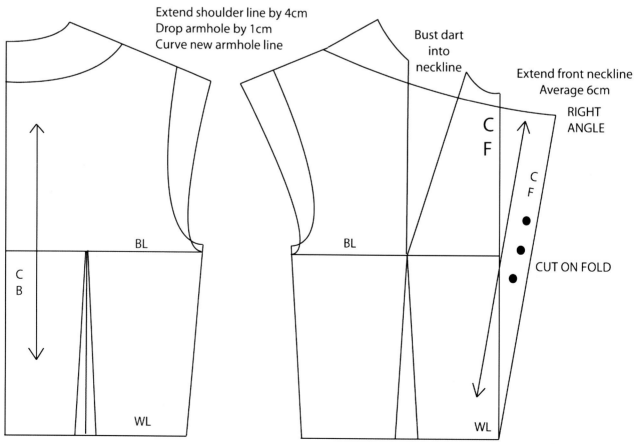

Extend shoulder line by 4cm
Drop armhole by 1cm
Curve new armhole line

Bust dart
into
neckline

Extend front neckline
Average 6cm

RIGHT
ANGLE

C
F

C
F

CUT ON FOLD

BL

BL

C
B

WL

WL

Gathered Neckline Plan

Gathered necklines work well in soft drapey fabric otherwise it creates a lot of stiffness in the design. The neckline needs to be opened in the one sided gathers principle to allow for the gathers. This way does not make the whole garment bigger. However if designing a smock or loose fitting style the whole garment can be made bigger using the two sided gathers principle.

The gathered neckline needs to have a facing behind the neckline, stitched in place and a draw cord threaded through for gathering the neckline. Button holes would be sewn at the CF point for the draw cord to be pulled through. Sample shown has an additional 5cm added into the neckline. For more gathers slash pattern open more to create finished look.

Back Bodice
Pivot side back bodice from BL outwards by 5cm
Extend shoulder 4cm
Drop armhole 1cm - reshape armhole
neckline - 12cm down CB to 6cm along shoulder. Facing 2.5cm width

Front Bodice
Pivot bust dart into neckline then extend by a further 5cm, pivoting the side bodice from BL outwards
Extend shoulder 4cm
Drop armhole 1cm and reshape armhole
Front neckline - drop neckline by 5cm and join to shoulder at 6cm along shoulder seam. Facing 2.5cm width

GATHERED NECKLINE

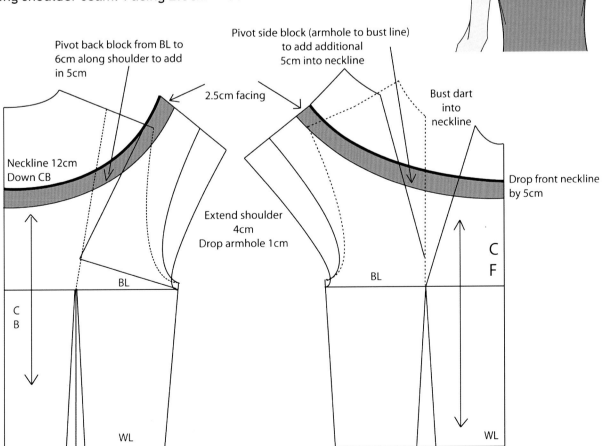

Pivot back block from BL to 6cm along shoulder to add in 5cm

Pivot side block (armhole to bust line) to add additional 5cm into neckline

2.5cm facing

Bust dart into neckline

Neckline 12cm Down CB

Extend shoulder 4cm
Drop armhole 1cm

Drop front neckline by 5cm

BL

BL

C B

C F

WL

WL

8. FRONT OPENINGS

Most blouses, shirts and jackets have a centre front opening. Even if the design is a-symmetrical or off centre with a front opening the following principles of creating the opening still apply. The front overlap for women's clothes always finish with the right side over the left side.

1.Facing

A facing is sewn on the inside of an edge which gives a clean finish. Average width of a facing is 4cm. Aswell as the facing a button stand needs to be added onto the front edge to allow for the buttons and button holes.

Front Bodice

Add button stand - the button stand width is determined by the size of the buttons you wish to use. For shirts and blouses buttons between 1cm and 2cm would generally be used. The buttonstand needs to be wider than this to allow for the button hole which is slightly bigger than the button. Button size plus 1cm is a good guide for button stand width.

The facing reaches the new front line then drops back by 4cm from CF line. Shoulder width would also be 4cm. Back neck facing would be 4cm all the way around the neckline.

Front Bodice Construction

Facing

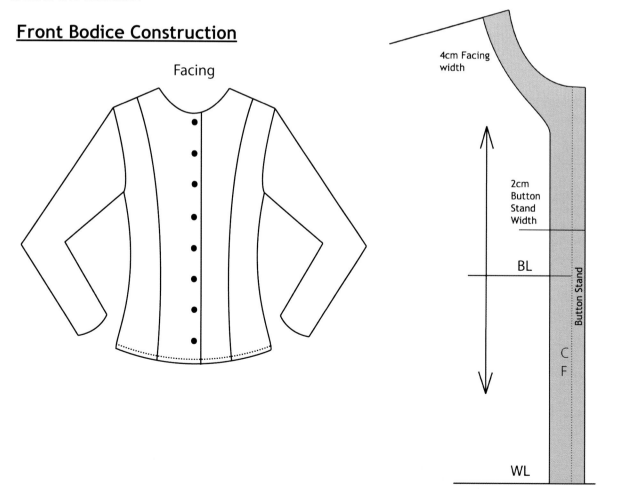

2. Edge to Edge Finishing

•Buttons and Loops

When finishing an edge with button and loops there is no need for a button stand as the front panels do not overlap. However a separate stand can be added to the left side bodice so that there is extra fabric behind the front closure when worn. A facing gives a nice finish on the inside.

Front bodice has a 4cm facing.
Back bodice would have the same 4cm facing.

Button and Loop

Front Bodice Construction

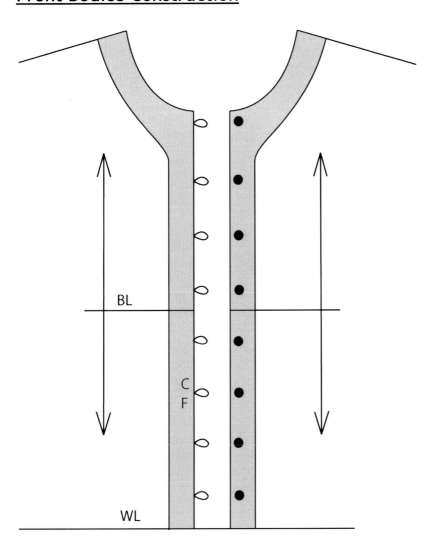

BL

C
F

WL

•Zipper

An open ended zipper can finish a front edge. However a separate stand can be added to the left side bodice so that there is extra fabric behind the front closure when worn.
A facing can be used on the inside - 4cm width around front and back neckline.

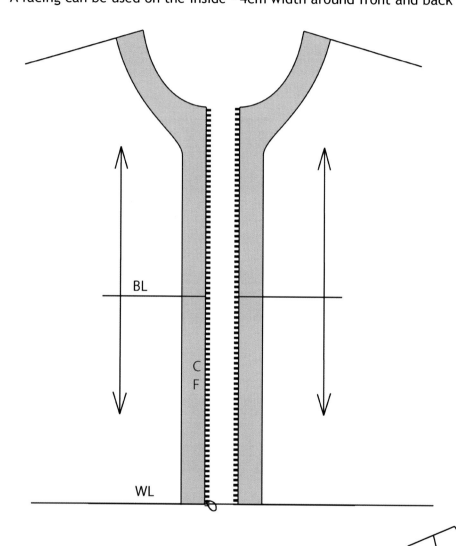

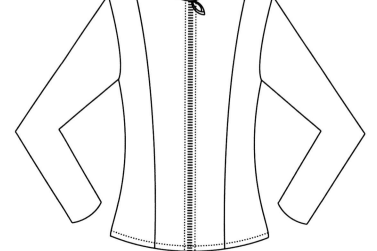

Zipper

3. Plackets

A placket is another way to open a garment. Traditionally used on shirts. It can be a seperate panel or added onto the bodice block. Most plackets will have topstiching detail to secure the placket in place.

Add button stand - the button stand width is determined by the size of the buttons you wish to use. For shirts and blouses buttons between 1cm and 2cm would generally be used. The buttonstand needs to be wider than this to allow for the button hole which is slightly bigger than the button. Button size plus 1cm is a good guide for button stand width.

•Grown on Placket

A grown on placket is an extension added to the Centre Front. Firstly you must add the button stand width, and then add the placket width. The grown on placket normally is folded to the inside of the front and stitched in place with the 1cm seam allowance being folded inside. However the placket can also be folded to the outside for design detail. This can only be done on some fabrics, as it is the inside of the fabric that will be seen and not the right side. It is also optional to stitch in place as when the buttons and button holes are attached to the front edge this will hold the placket in place.

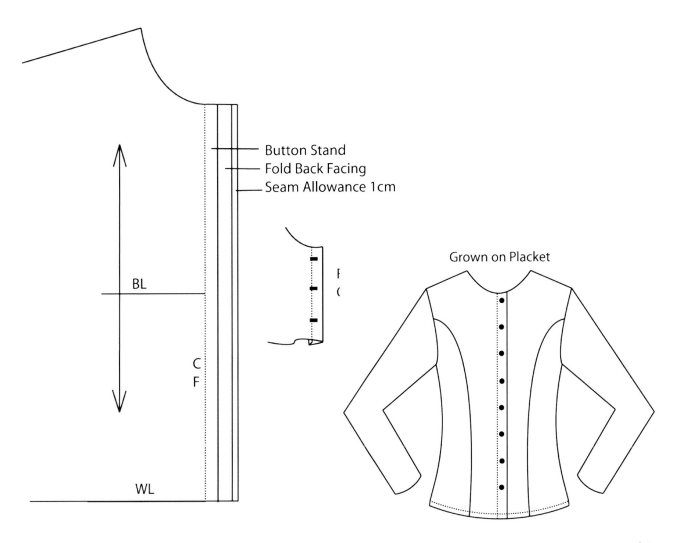

Grown on Placket

•Concealed Placket

A concealed placket has a separate panel behind the right side CF edge where the buttonholes sit. The CF edge needs to have a button stand and fold back added (same principle as grown on placket) plus the separate panel on the right side only, which is twice the width of the button stand. The separate panel is sewn to the right side for women's wear, and buttonholes added onto it. The left side has the buttons.

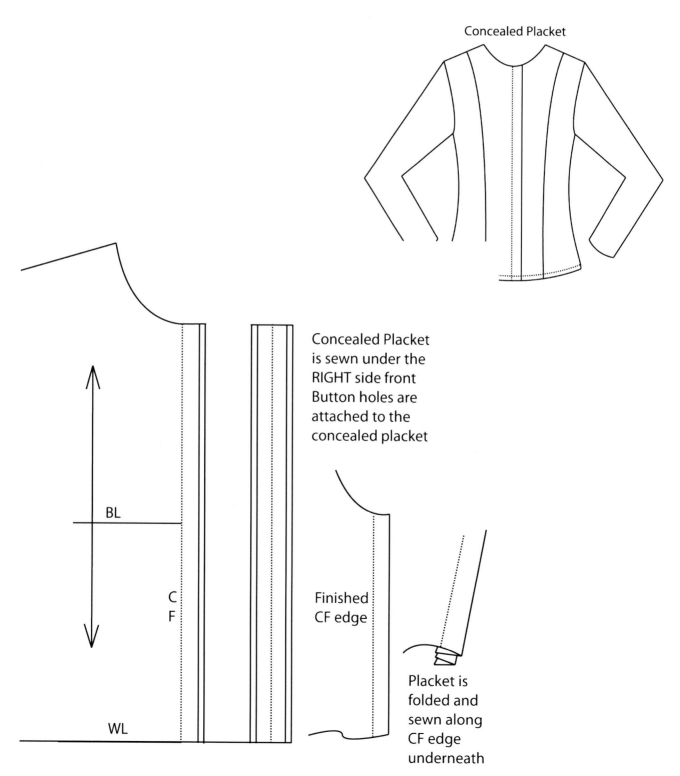

Concealed Placket

Concealed Placket is sewn under the RIGHT side front Button holes are attached to the concealed placket

BL

C
F

WL

Finished CF edge

Placket is folded and sewn along CF edge underneath

•Separate Placket

A separate placket is constructed by taking the button stand measurement – adding seam and cutting one on fold. Left side placket is hidden underneath the right side placket so can either be a separate panel or a grown on placket. Separate plackets work well if your design uses different fabric for the placket.

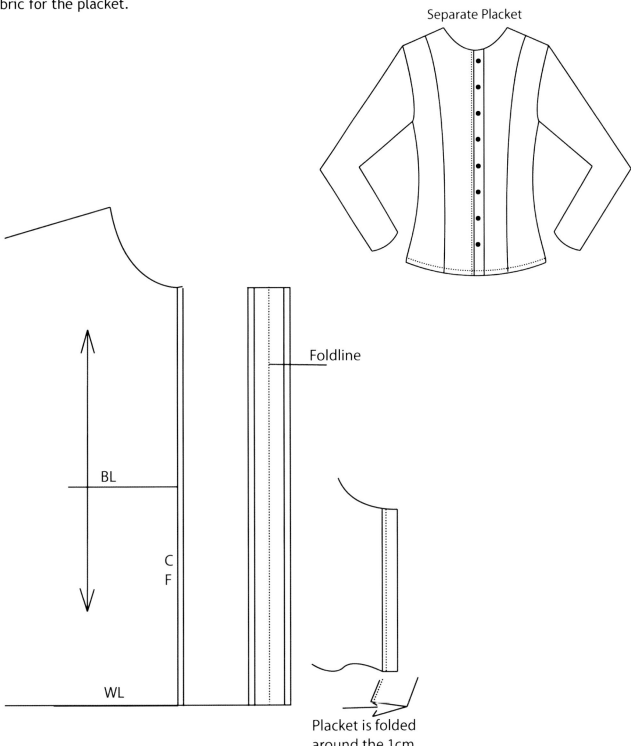

Separate Placket

Foldline

BL

C F

WL

Placket is folded around the 1cm CF seam allowance

•Lip Placket

A lip is an extension, which is fixed at one side. A "LIP" placket is the same construction as a separate placket but adding in a lip on both edges of the placket. For construction, one of the lips is added to the left side, while the other to the centre of the placket. So when folded the lips sit on each side of the finished placket. A lip measurement is generally 1cm but can be wider. The under placket is the same construction as a grown on placket.

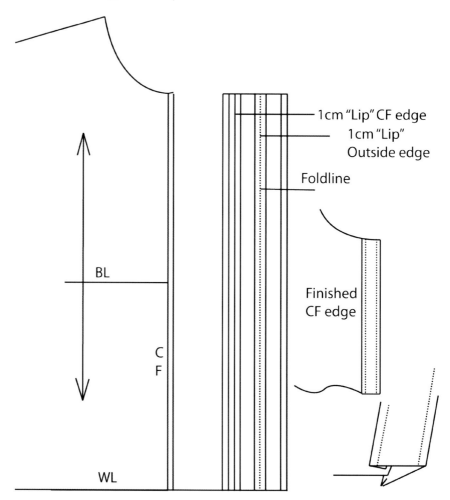

BL

CF

WL

1cm "Lip" CF edge
1cm "Lip" Outside edge
Foldline
Finished CF edge

** Sew under edge first turn and stitch 1cm lip on RIGHT side of garment. Stitch outside lip 1cm

Lip Placket

4. Double Breasted Front Opening

Double-breasted finish is the same as a facing finish but with a wider button stand to allow for two rows of buttons. A double-breasted finish is generally used on jackets and coats, although it can be used on shirts and blouses. Average finish is a 4cm button stand – which gives an 8cm overlap. Although the maximum overlap would be 8cm – 16cm finish.

** It is not advisable to overlap more than a total of 16cm otherwise the button stand interferes with the waist and bust dart body shaping.

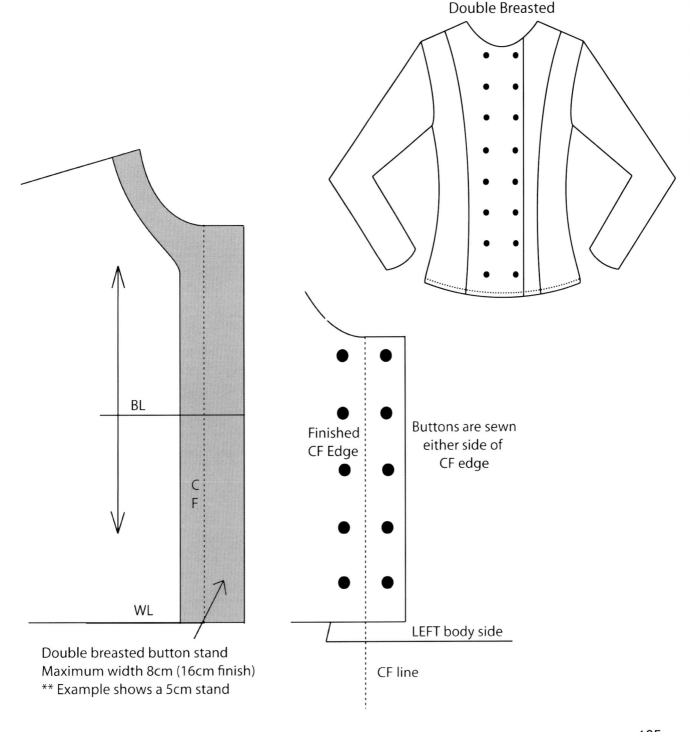

Double Breasted

BL

C F

WL

Double breasted button stand
Maximum width 8cm (16cm finish)
** Example shows a 5cm stand

Finished CF Edge

Buttons are sewn either side of CF edge

LEFT body side

CF line

9. COLLARS

Types of Collars

Collars are attached to the neckline of garments. There are four different types of collar construction. The key measurement when making a collar is the neckline.
Every collar has a style line – this is the outside edge and can be styled as per design requirements.

There are 4 main types of collars –

1.Flat collars
Flat collars sit on the neckline, lying flat against the bodice. The outside edge of the collar is your style line.

2.Grown on collars
This collar is constructed as an extension of the bodice. The break line on a grown on collar is the line where the collar folds back on itself. This line is then extended at the shoulder to add the back neck measurement so that the collar has a CB seam only. This collar is used on all blouses, shirts, jackets and coats. It is a soft collar which sits flat against the bodice with a slight rise at the back neck.

3.Standing Collars
Collars that stand around the neckline and do not sit on the bodice. Shirt collars, mandarin collar, standing collars. Standing collars can be made as two pattern pieces – a collar stand and a collar fall, or as a one piece pattern.When making a standing collar from two pattern pieces the collar fall is 1cm larger than the collar stand to allow the fall to drape over the stand, and therefore hiding the seam joining to the bodice.

4.Collar with Rever
Rever collars are traditional tailoring collars and can be found on most coats and tailored jackets, in menswear and women's wear. A rever collar is two collars, the bottom collar is called the lapel. A break line shows the finished length of the lapel on the bodice.Then a second, the top collar is added joining it onto the lapel. Both the top collar and lapel can be any shape or design. The lapel sits on top of the bodice, and the top collar stands up around the back of the neck.

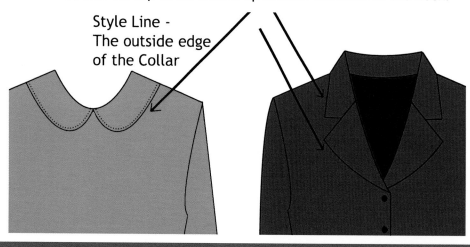

Style Line -
The outside edge
of the Collar

FASHION DESIGN

Measuring the Neckline

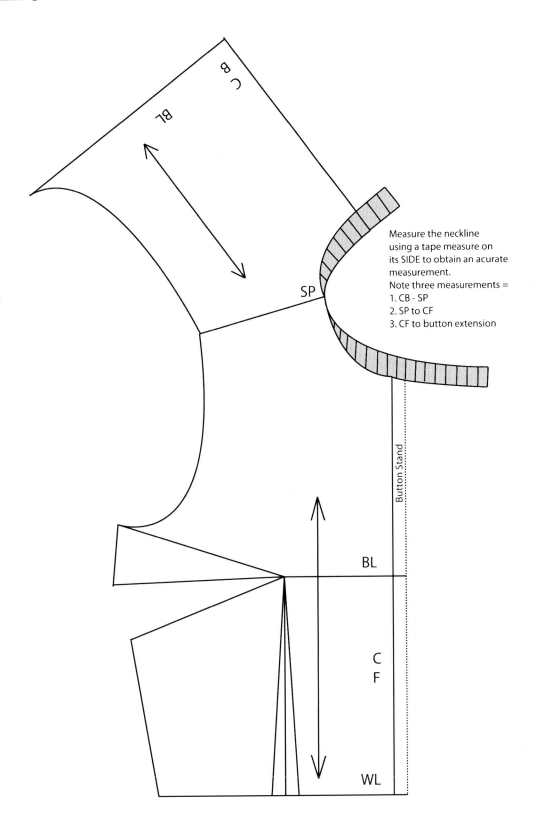

Measure the neckline using a tape measure on its SIDE to obtain an acurate measurement.
Note three measurements =
1. CB - SP
2. SP to CF
3. CF to button extension

FASHION DESIGN

1. Flat Collars

Flat collars sit on top of the bodice. You would cut 2 pieces of the collar and sew them together before attaching the collar to the neckline of the bodice.

a. Peter Pan Collar

A Peter Pan collar is an old-fashioned collar style generally used on soft blouses. An average of 6cm wide with a rounded front finish it can also made with lace or trims attached to the style line.

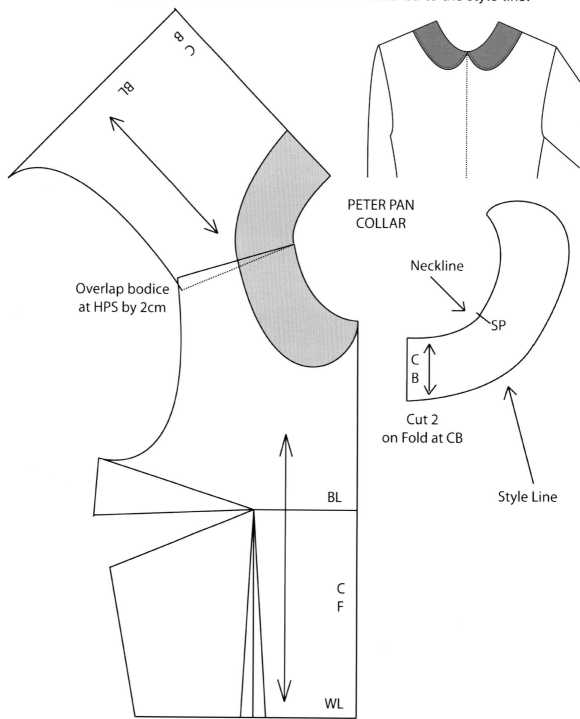

Overlap bodice at HPS by 2cm

PETER PAN COLLAR

Neckline

SP

C B

Cut 2 on Fold at CB

Style Line

BL

CF

WL

b. Sailor Collar

A sailor collar is a big wide collar that sits over the top bodice and shoulder, falling down the back of the bodice block. A sailor collar generally overlaps the sleeve head by an average of 3cm. Square on the back it can also have a tie to finish the centre front edge.

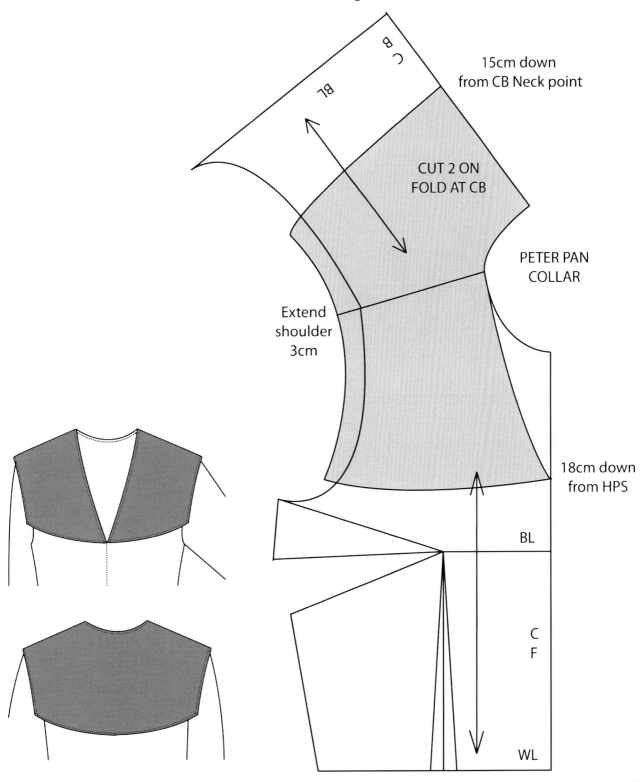

CB

BL

15cm down
from CB Neck point

CUT 2 ON
FOLD AT CB

PETER PAN
COLLAR

Extend
shoulder
3cm

18cm down
from HPS

BL

C
F

WL

c. Flat Collar with Low Neckline

A flat collar only has a CB seam, where the shoulder seam is joined to create one piece. The collar can be as high or low as required on the front bodice. You can also drop the back neckline if you require a lower back neck with collar. To enable the flat collar to sit comfortably over the bodice the style line must be slashed 4 times around the neck and 1cm added into each section. This will allow the collar to sit comfortably over the bodice. This collar is cut 2 pieces and joined together before attaching it to the neckline.

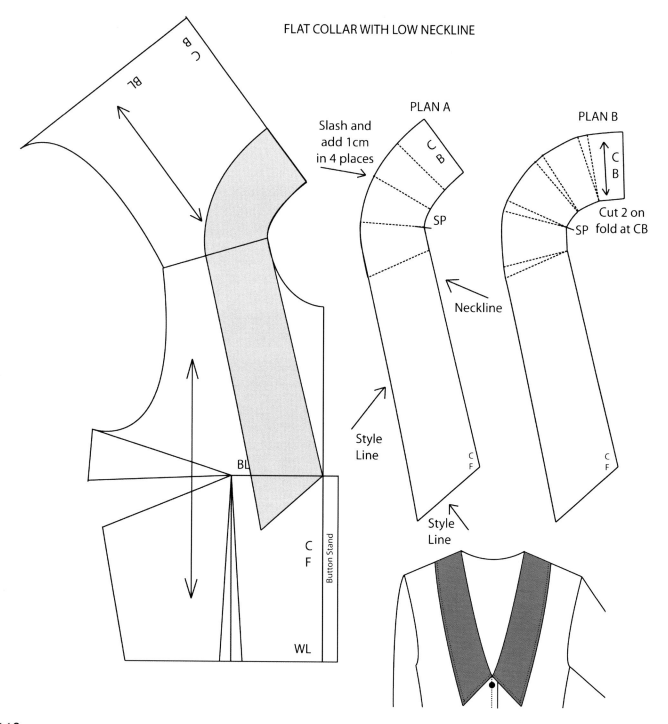

FLAT COLLAR WITH LOW NECKLINE

Slash and add 1cm in 4 places

PLAN A

PLAN B

Cut 2 on fold at CB

Neckline

Style Line

Style Line

d. Frill Flat Collar

Using the same principle as the flat collar - the collar is spread and the frill added into the style line, the one side gathers principle. The frill can be as full (wide) as required. If making a very wide frill a circle is the largest one piece pattern that can be made unless you use a seam at the shoulder

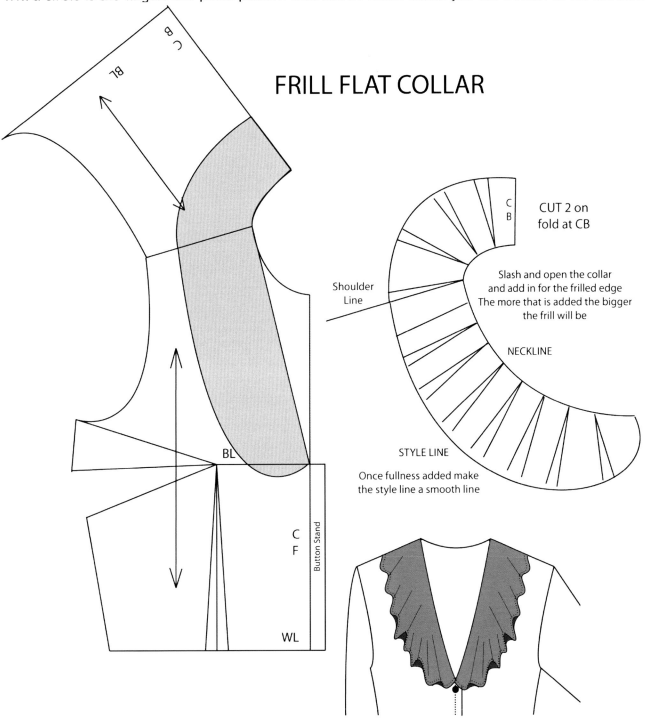

FRILL FLAT COLLAR

CUT 2 on
fold at CB

Slash and open the collar
and add in for the frilled edge
The more that is added the bigger
the frill will be

NECKLINE

Shoulder
Line

STYLE LINE

Once fullness added make
the style line a smooth line

111

e. Cape Collar

A cape collar is joined at the neckline and falls down the front and back bodice, draping over the arm. The cape collar can be as wide as a full circle by slashing through the body and adding in one sided gathers principle. The shoulder length is shorter than the CF and CB length to allow the cape to appear the same length when worn. Cape collar necklines are finished with a facing on the inside. A cape style of collar can be just Cut 1 piece with a double turn or binding at the hemline.

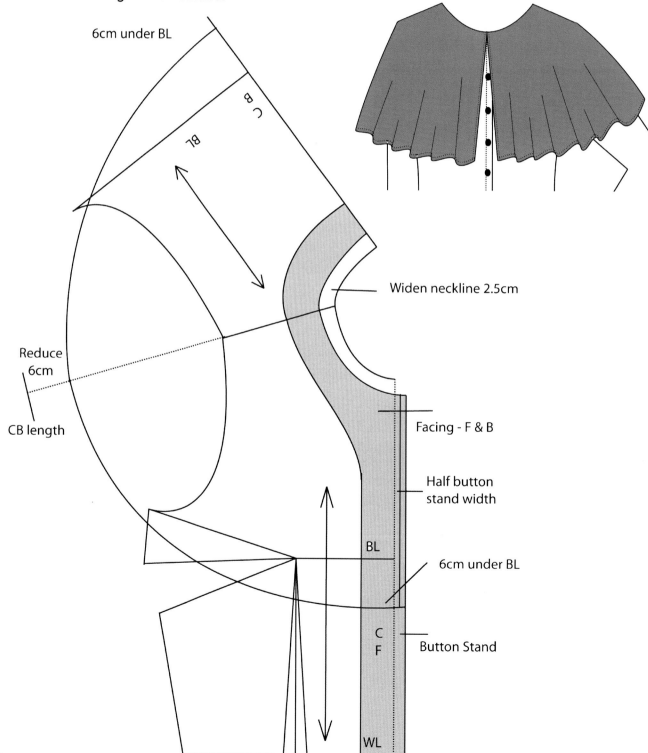

6cm under BL

CB

BL

Reduce 6cm

CB length

Widen neckline 2.5cm

Facing - F & B

Half button stand width

BL

6cm under BL

C F

Button Stand

WL

2. Grown on Collars

Shawl Collar

A shawl collar is also a flat collar which sits over the bodice, but instead of a separate piece it is added onto the bodice block. A break line is drawn for the length of the collar, then extended at the shoulder seam to add the back neck measurement. The break line is where the collar is folded back on itself.Made with a facing, it is the facing that is seen when the garment is worn. A shawl collar is used on blouses through to jackets and coats.

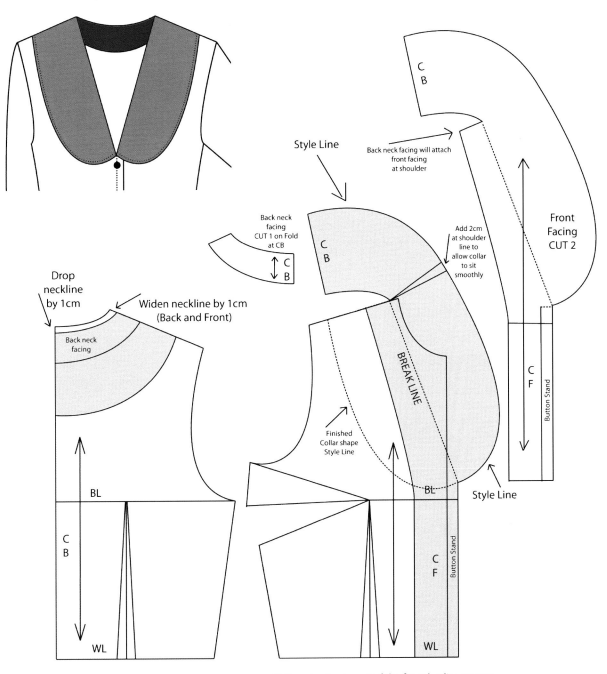

** Shawl collar is part of the front bodice pattern

3. Standing Collars

a. Mandarin Collar

A mandarin collar, or also known as a Nehru collar is a standing collar – or the "collar stand" of a shirt collar. The style line (top edge and CF edge) can be any shape. Generally 4cm in height as the higher the collar becomes it requires more shape to fit into the neckline. The neckline is measured and a rectangle created. This needs to be slashed and made smaller at the style line to allow for it to fit into the neckline. For designs where the collar is required to sit straight and away from the neckline, do not reduce the top edge, instead keep the collar as a rectangle shape.

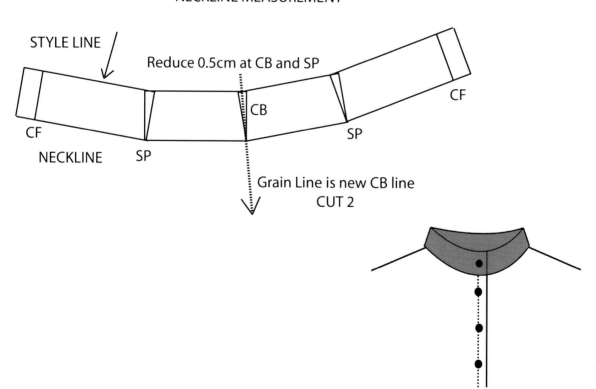

MANDARIN COLLAR

b. One Piece Shirt Collar

A one piece shirt collar is a cheaper method of creating a shirt collar. It does not sit as firm or straight as a two piece shirt collar due to no central seam for the collar to fold back on itself. The finished look is flat at the centre front, standing up the neckline at the back.

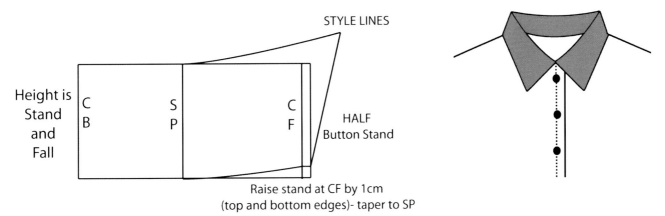

ONE PIECE COLLAR

Height is Stand and Fall

STYLE LINES

C B

S P

C F

HALF Button Stand

Raise stand at CF by 1cm (top and bottom edges)- taper to SP

NECKLINE MEASUREMENT

c. Convertible Collar

Using the same method as the one piece shirt collar, a small collar stand is taken from the back and into the front neckline. This gives a "flat" collar at the front but allows for the collar to stand more firm at the CB as it has a fixed seam to fold over.

It looks the same from the front as the one piece shirt collar.

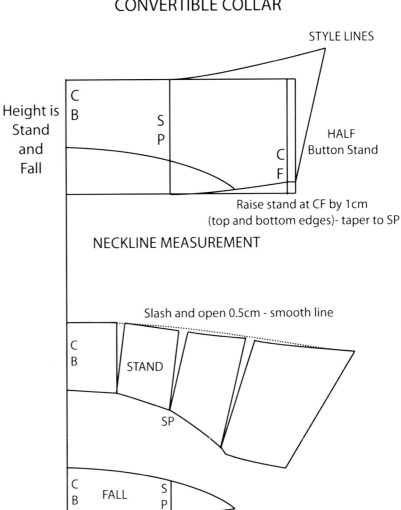

CONVERTIBLE COLLAR

STYLE LINES

Height is Stand and Fall

C B

S P

C F

HALF Button Stand

Raise stand at CF by 1cm (top and bottom edges)- taper to SP

NECKLINE MEASUREMENT

Slash and open 0.5cm - smooth line

C B

STAND

SP

C B

FALL

S P

d. Shirt Collar

A shirt collar is made of two pattern pieces. The collar stand with a collar fall attached to the top edge. When creating a shirt collar the fall needs to be 1cm larger than the stand to allow for the collar to fall over the stand and the seam be hidden. If the fall is much larger than 1cm it will not sit so neatly against the collar stand. The style line on a shirt collar can be adapted as per design requirements. This collar stands up from the neckline, with the collar fall coming down onto the bodice at the front.

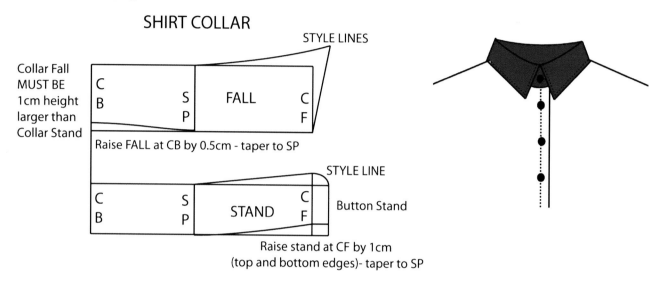

SHIRT COLLAR

Collar Fall MUST BE 1cm height larger than Collar Stand

Raise FALL at CB by 0.5cm - taper to SP

Raise stand at CF by 1cm
(top and bottom edges)- taper to SP

NECKLINE MEASUREMENT

e. Double Shirt Collar

To create a double collar the same method as the shirt collar is used but instead of one FALL there are two. The purpose of this design is to have two FALL's that are different – either in fabric, shape or colour. Both collar falls are sewn individually, then attached together into the collar stand.

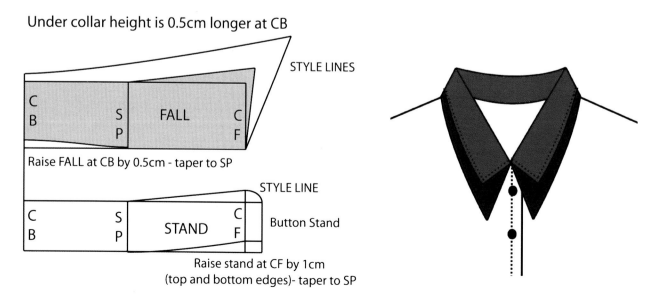

Under collar height is 0.5cm longer at CB

Raise FALL at CB by 0.5cm - taper to SP

Raise stand at CF by 1cm
(top and bottom edges)- taper to SP

NECKLINE MEASUREMENT

4. Rever Collars

Rever collars are traditional tailoring collars and used mainly on jackets and coats. It is a two piece collar where part of the collar, the lapel, is an extension to the front bodice. The top collar is a separate pattern piece. As all collars the style lines can be shaped as per design. The break point creates the length of the lapel at the centre front. The break line is where the collar will fold back on itself and sit on the bodice panel. The top collar can come to any point down the rever as per design. A rever collar creates a lapel covering the front bodice and the top collar standing around the back neckline. Rever collars can be wide and open at the neckline or close to the neck.

Rever Collar Terminology

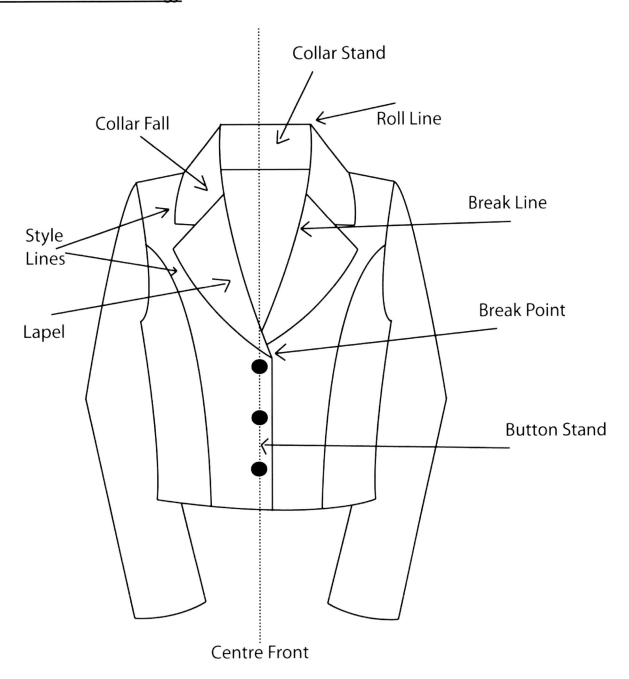

FASHION DESIGN

a. Rever Collar

Rever Collars have two collars - the top collar and the lapel. Both can be designed with different style lines and sizes. Rever Collar, and Rever Collar B are two typical rever collar styles with different collar shapes, break points and top collar sizes. When creating a rever collar firstly you must add your button stand onto the centre front panel. Coat and jacket buttons tend to be larger than shirts and blouses. A common size is 2.5cm. Therefore a 3.5cm button stand should be added.

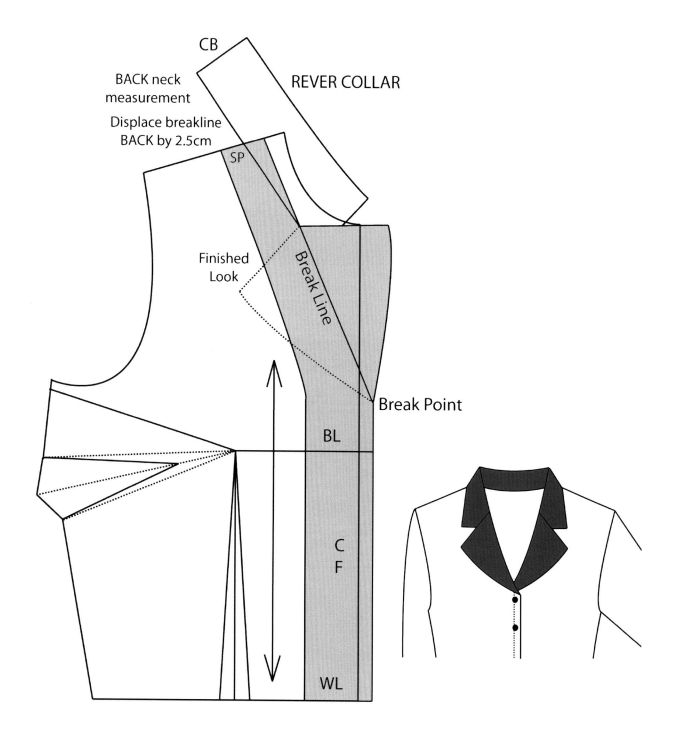

CB

BACK neck measurement

Displace breakline BACK by 2.5cm

REVER COLLAR

SP

Break Line

Finished Look

Break Point

BL

C F

WL

FASHION DESIGN

b. Rever Collar (B)

This rever collar has a different lapel and top collar shape. The position where the top collar joins the lapel can be anywhere down the length of the lapel.

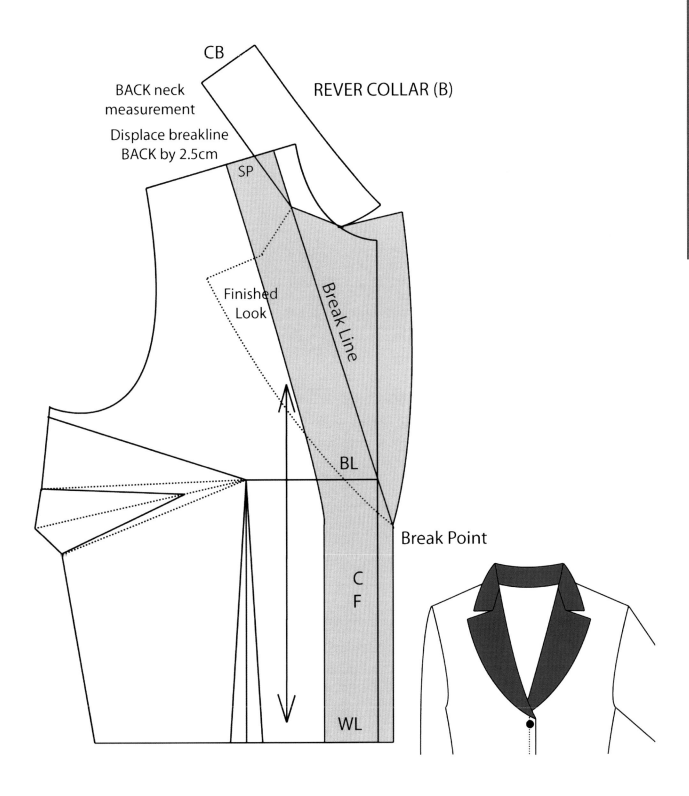

FASHION DESIGN

c. Double Breasted Rever Collar

Double breasted rever collars are commonly seen on coats, to give extra width and warmth at the front. Constructed in exactly the same way as a single breasted rever collar, but with additional button stand added first to allow for the double breasted finish.

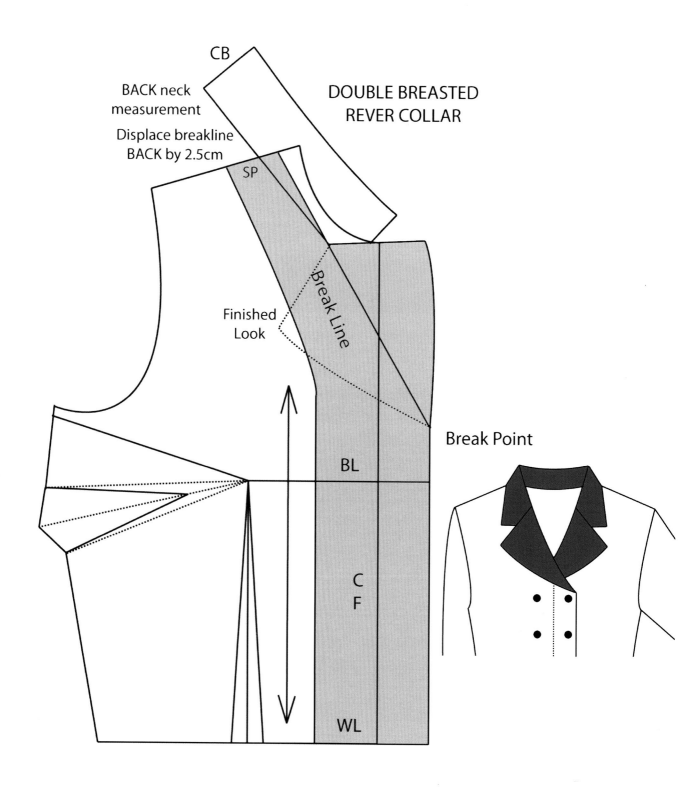

CB

BACK neck measurement

Displace breakline BACK by 2.5cm

SP

DOUBLE BREASTED REVER COLLAR

Break Line

Finished Look

Break Point

BL

C F

WL

FASHION DESIGN

Standing Collar Sample Designs

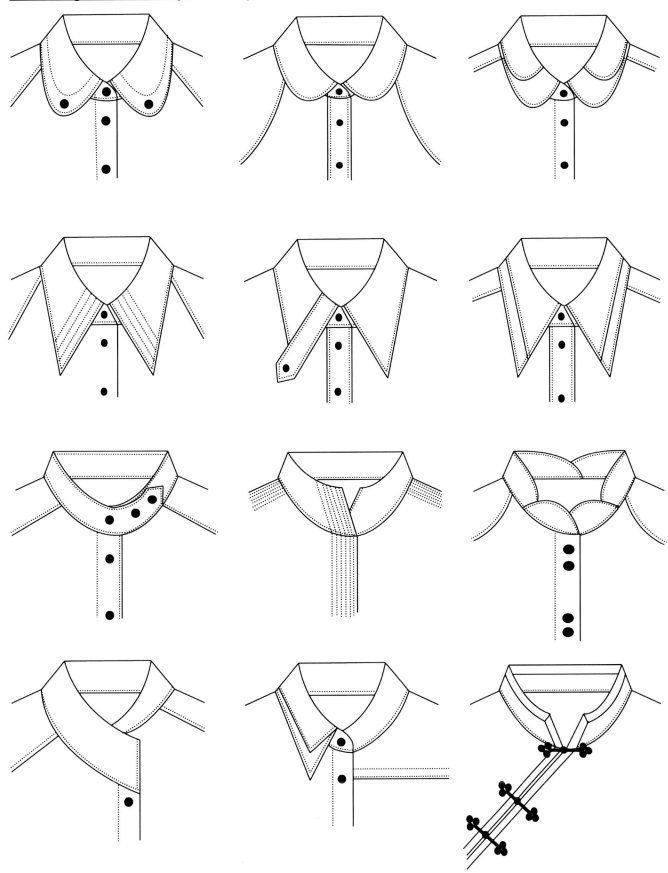

FASHION
DESIGN

Standing Collar Sample Designs

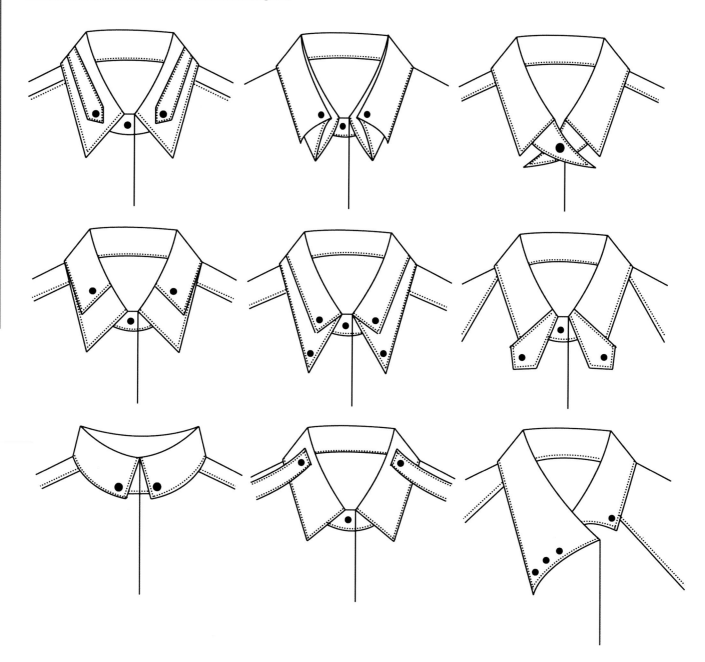

FASHION DESIGN

Back Collar Sample Designs

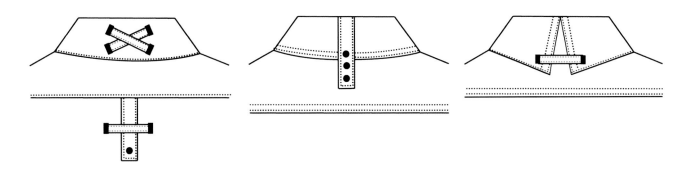

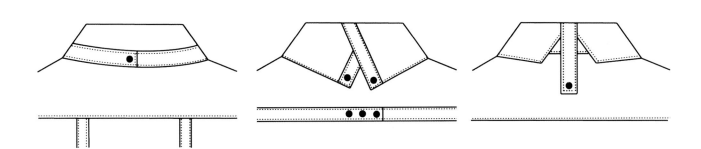

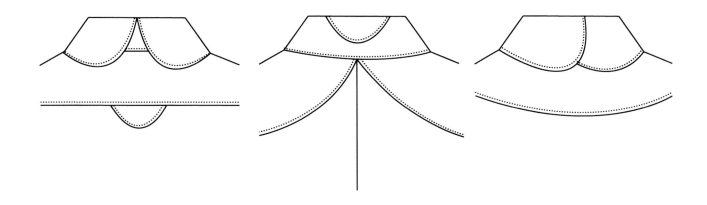

FASHION DESIGN

10. SHIRT DETAILS

Shirts are constructed with a variety of different pattern pieces where the designer is able to create 100's of designs. Shirts can also be made in a variety of fabrics, from fine chiffons to heavy cottons.

Block
Fitted shirts use either the panel line or princess line block
Loose fitting shirts using the loose fitting block
Semi fitted would use a smaller waist dart and the bust dart

Sleeve and Cuff
Any type of sleeve can be used on a shirt. A traditional shirt would have a cuff and placket design on the end of the sleeve.

Shoulder detailing - Yoke and Epelets
Most traditional shirts will have a back neck yoke cut out of the bodice block. 2cm from the front bodice and down to the XB on the back bodice. Join the yoke at the shoulder seam, creating a new shoulder seam dropped onto the front bodice where the yoke meets the front panels. Yoke's can be made into many different designs– pleats, gathers, shoulder tabs etc. Some shirt designs have a front yoke and a back yoke – keeping the shoulder seam in the same position.
On the shoulder line an epelet can be placed on casual shirts. An epelet is constructed the same as a waistband, either cutting straight on the fold, or if curved cutting two pieces. Epelets finish 1cm before neckline point and can be fixed into the shoulder seam.

Bodice design
A closure needs to be added to shirts. Centre front button stand using a placket is also a traditional shirt closure. However buttons and loops, zippers and facings can be used also. Front openings also do not have to be at the CF. A-Symmetric designs also work well on shirts. Hemlines at the side seam (or any panel) can also have detail.

Pockets
Generally patch pockets are placed over the bust area on casual shirts. Shirts can also be designed with tailored pockets - jet and welts - however this gives extra bulk on the inside so not as commonly seen as patch pockets.

Collars - all types of collars can be used on shirts. Even the back of a top collar (collar fall) can be designed.

Shirt Design Details:-

Collar
Back collar
Placket
Yoke
Epelet
Sleeve
Cuff, Cuff placket
Pocket
Side hem detail

FASHION DESIGN

Back Neck Yoke Designs

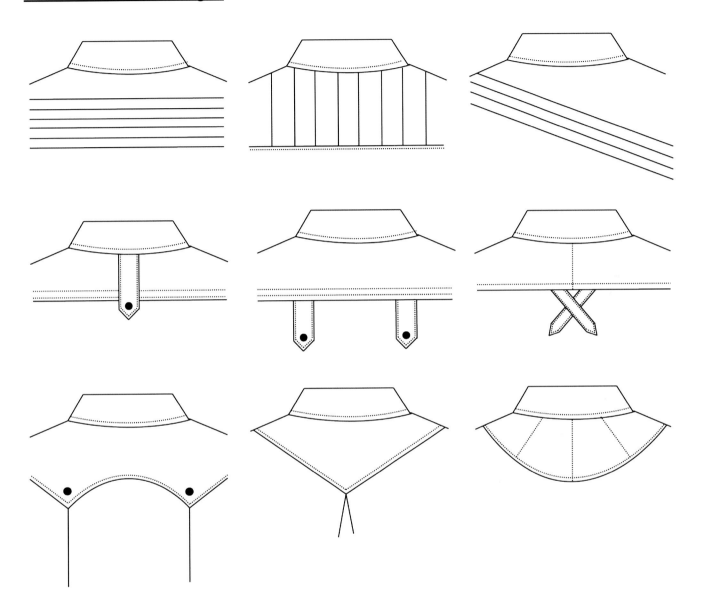

FASHION DESIGN

Shoulder Epelet Designs

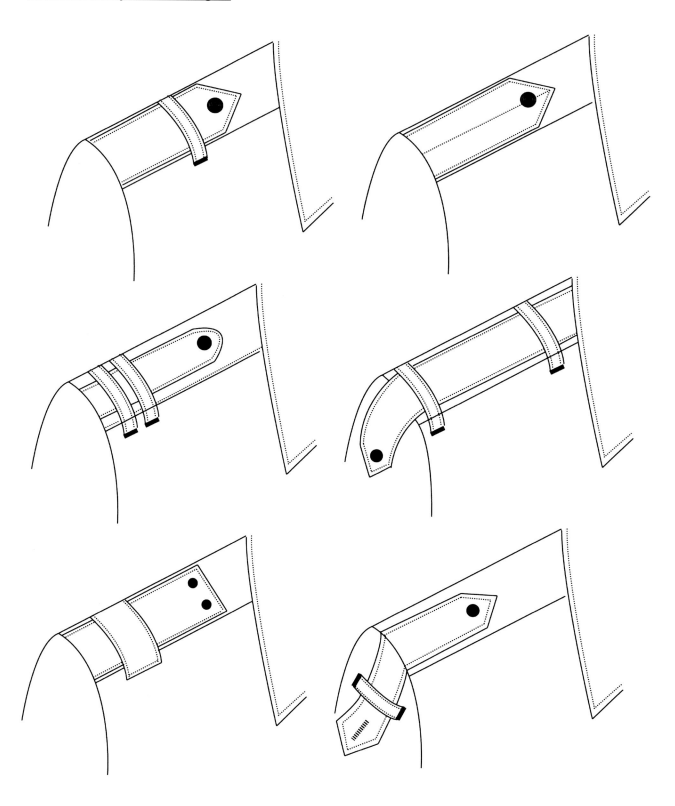

FASHION DESIGN

Side Hem Design Details

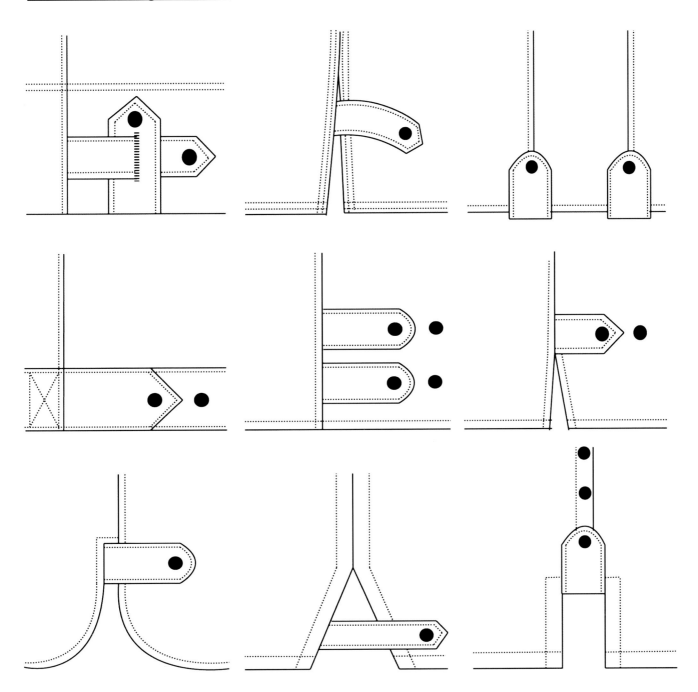

Shirt Sample Designs

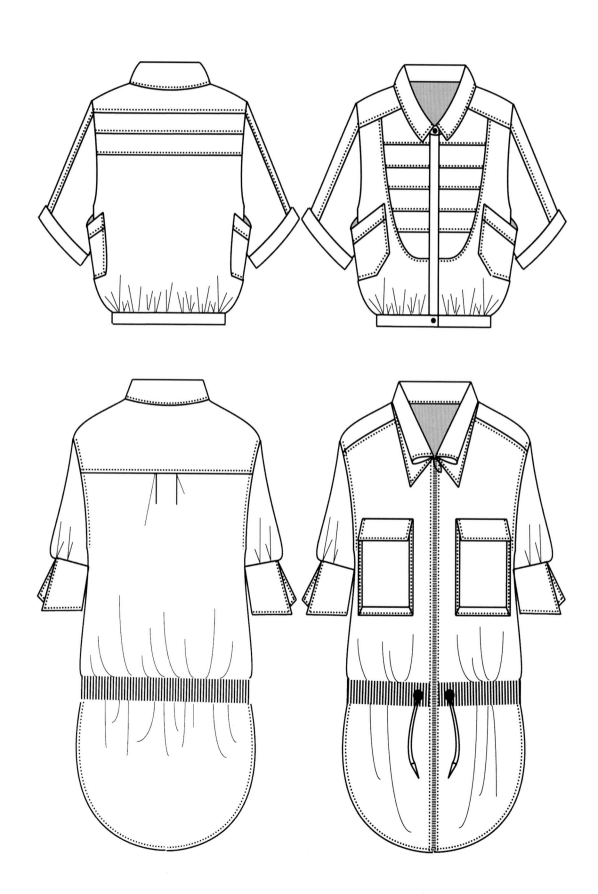

FASHION DESIGN

Shirt Sample Designs

11. HOODS

A hood can be attached to any size of neckline. The smallest hood must have an 18cm back neck width to enable it to sit comfortably around the neckline. The wider the neck measurement the more the hood will fall down against the bodice. Most hoods raise up the head from the neckline, therefore the neckline measurement must equal the total head width. There are two basic hood shapes – the basic hood which is straight at the centre front so would give more coverage over the face. The shaped hood is angled in at the front and would therefore expose more of the face when worn up. A hood pattern can be cut into panels and re-designed according to the finished garment design. A hood height needs to cover the head comfortably. The average head size is 30.8cm, which is three quarters of neck to waist measurement. Hoods can be much higher than the head, this will cause draping around the base when the hood is worn up.

Basic Hood

The traditional hood height is 3/4's of the neck to waist measurement PLUS 6cm.
The bottom width of the hood is the neck measurement
Raise the centre back of the hood by 6cm – draw a straight line down to the centre front, the length of the neck measurement.
Angle the line by raising it 0.5cm between the centre back and shoulder point, and dropping by 1cm from shoulder point to centre front.
Curve the hood out at the back of the head by 2cm and join with a smooth curve.

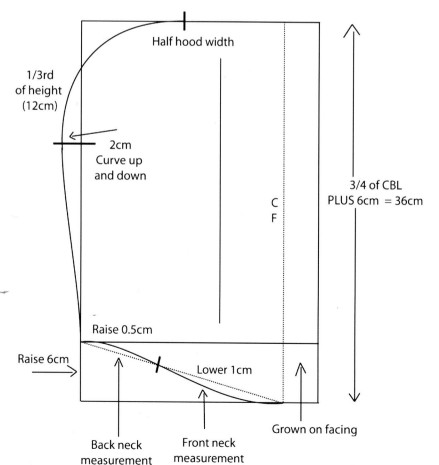

Extend out from the centre front line for the facing to finish the front neck edge. The facing inside edge can be finished with binding, or over locked.

The facing can always be a separate panel, attaching at the CF.

Shaped Hood

Copy the method of the basic hood then shape the front edge :-
Reduce from CF line (1/3rd up from neckline) by 3cm - curve down to the 6cm line above neckline
Drop the top front of hood by 1.5cm, curve line towards centre of head and down the CF line.
Button Stand attaches to CF body panel (only use if bodice has a button stand)
Facing to finish - 4cm width. Edge stitch 1mm on inside. Separate panel as line is curved.

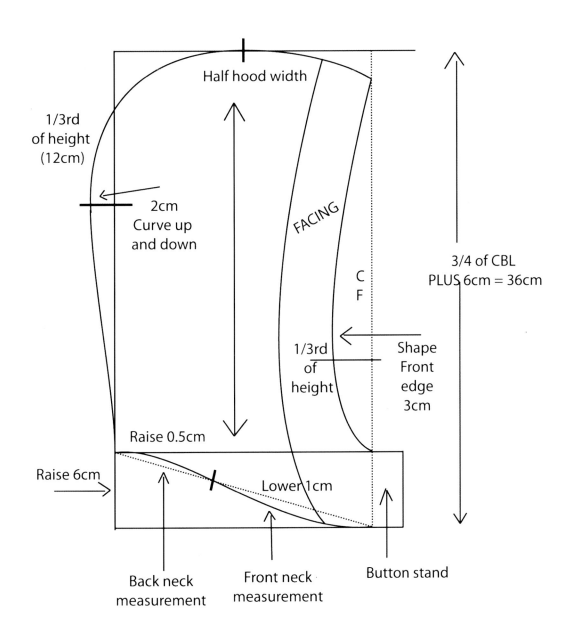

FASHION DESIGN

Hood with Gusset

To add a gusset into the hood you must reduce the hood neck measurement and around the head to accommodate the width of the gusset. Using the basic or shaped hood pattern reduce the hood half the gusset width. Create the gusset and shape over the back of the head. The widest gusset width would be the width of the head – around 14cm.

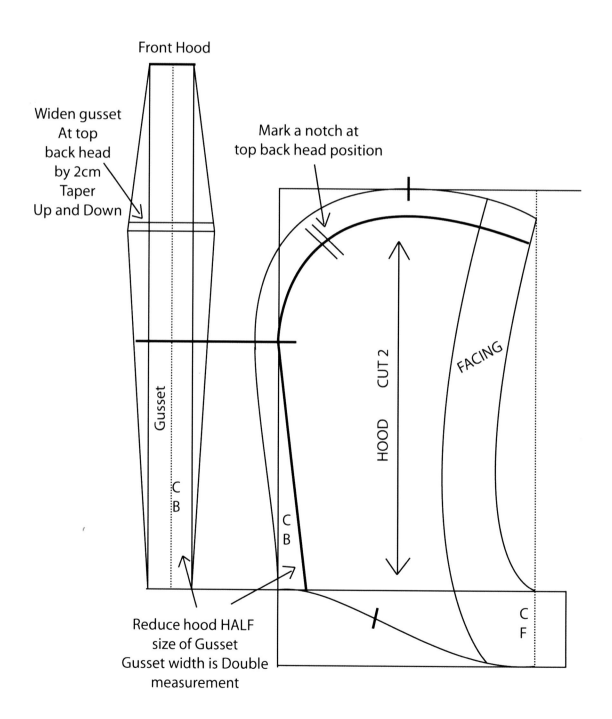

Front Hood

Widen gusset
At top
back head
by 2cm
Taper
Up and Down

Mark a notch at
top back head position

Gusset

C B

HOOD   CUT 2

FACING

CUT 2

C B

C F

Reduce hood HALF
size of Gusset
Gusset width is Double
measurement

FASHION DESIGN

Hood Designs

Hood Designs constructed with the Basic Hood Pattern

Design 1 - wide open neckline with neck panel. Hood is attached to back only.
Design 2 - hood does not go over the head. This type of design can be classed as a grown on collar also. It has a top panel which folds back down on itself.

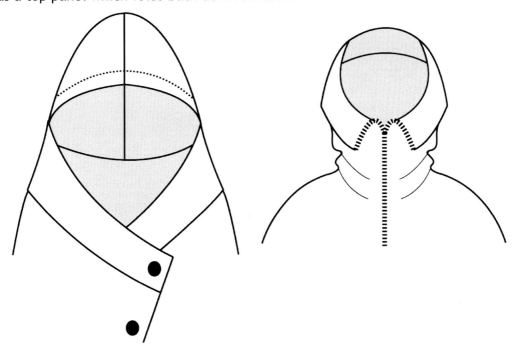

Hood Designs constructed with the Shaped Hood Pattern

Design 3 - Shaped hood with gusset. No button stand as the design has a zipper front closure.
Design 4 - Shaped hood, extra high and wide to cause draping effect when down.

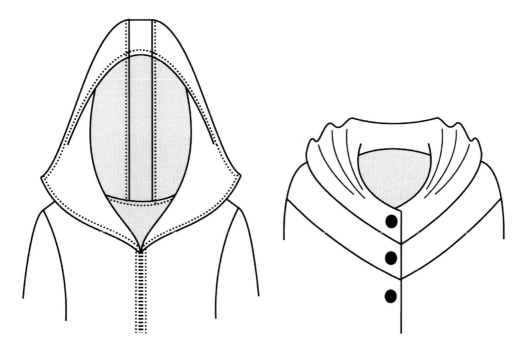

12. JUMPSUIT BLOCK

A jumpsuit block is made by combining the bodice block with the trouser block. The most important measurement on a jumpsuit is the body length – too long or short will cause the crutch line to not sit in the correct position. Depending on a person's height will determin their body length. Jumpsuits are a difficult garment to achieve a perfect fit as if the crutch line (between the legs) is too high or low it is uncomfortable to wear. When designing jumpsuits a dropped crutch line would accomodate more body lengths.

Jumpsuit's are an item of clothing that comes in and out of fashion in women's wear. Common all the time only in children's wear.

Jumpsuit Block Construction

Place basic bodice block over the top of the trouser block matching at the waistline.
Trace around from waistline to shoulder line.
The back bodice will not be straight as the back waist of the trousers is angled.
Smooth all seams - CB, CF and side seam.
Match the body darts - continue from the bodice darts, re-angling the back waist dart to ensure it is a straight line.

Jumpsuit
Block

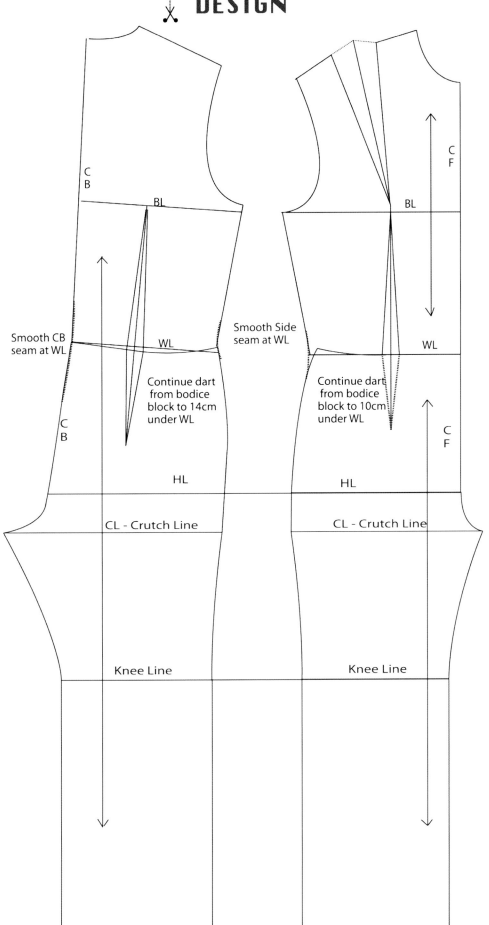

C
B

BL

C
F

Smooth CB
seam at WL

WL

Smooth Side
seam at WL

BL

WL

C
B

Continue dart
from bodice
block to 14cm
under WL

Continue dart
from bodice
block to 10cm
under WL

C
F

HL

HL

CL - Crutch Line

CL - Crutch Line

Knee Line

Knee Line

Jumpsuit Design

The jumpsuit design is a young casual summer design, made in a cotton or linen fabric. The bust dart has been moved into the princess line position.

Bodice

1.   Length – 16cm under HL
2.   Plus 3cm at CB inside leg, 1cm at side seam – taper to CL
3.   Plus 2cm at CF inside leg, 1cm at side seam – taper to CL
4.   Extend princess line to new hemline Back and Front
5.   Mark a point 3cm below BL at CB -take across to side seam, 1cm under BL
6.   Drop back neck 3cm, shoulder at 6cm – draw new back neckline (for hood)
7.   Back neckline facing – 4cm width
8.   Shoulder is 6cm, drop front neckline 5cm – connect with a curve and extend 2cm for button stand
9.   Add CF button stand – 2cm width – neckline to 18cm under WL.
10.   Curve new armhole line – 4cm down neckline to finish 1cm under BL
11.   Front neckline facing is 4cm wide

Hood

1.   Using basic hood block extend neckline measurement to bodice measurement. Mark two notches – one for back neck measurement, the second 4cm along (front neckline position)
2.   Hood height is 35cm (longer than block to increase drape when down)
3.   Curve new back neckline measurement
4.   Add 2cm button stand

Jumpsuit Design Plan

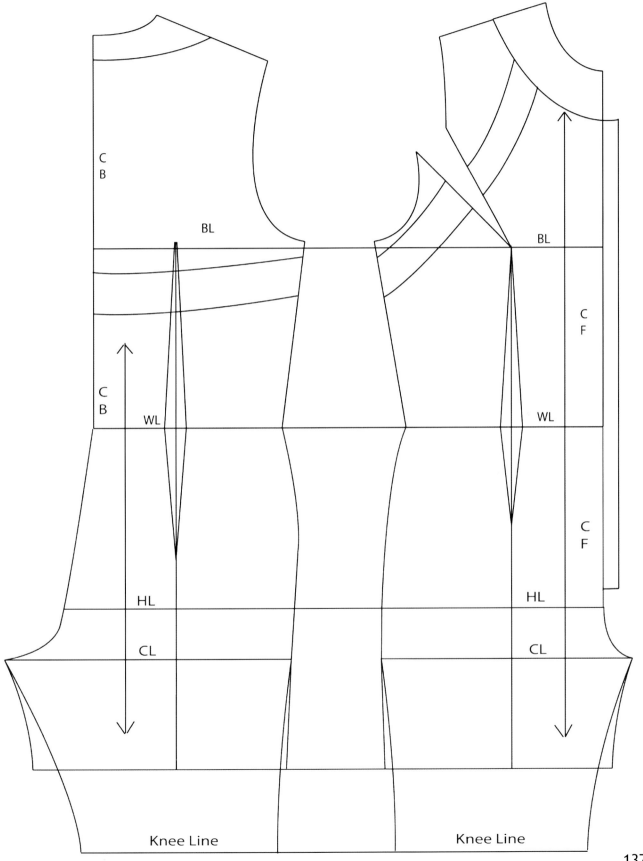

FASHION DESIGN

Jumpsuit Design Pattern

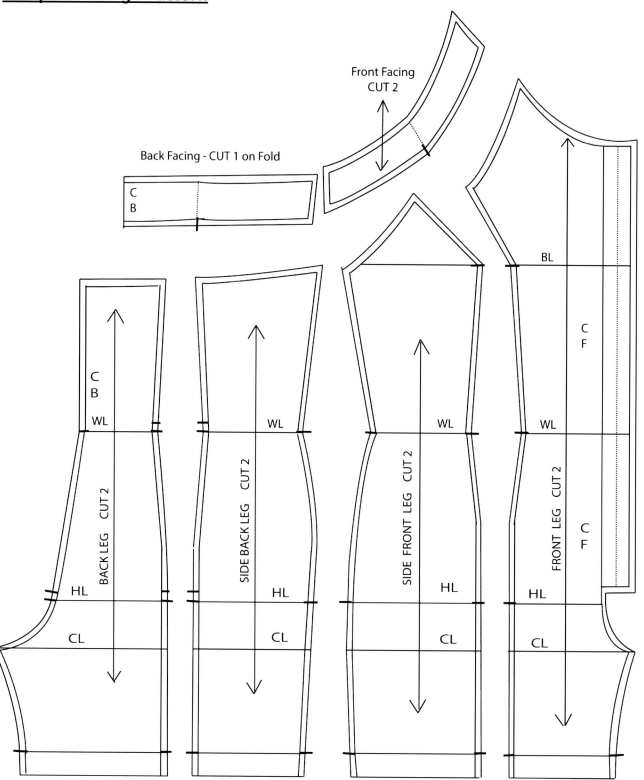

Front Facing
CUT 2

Back Facing - CUT 1 on Fold

C
B

C
B

WL

BACK LEG   CUT 2

HL

CL

WL

SIDE BACK LEG   CUT 2

HL

CL

WL

SIDE FRONT LEG   CUT 2

HL

CL

BL

C
F

WL

FRONT LEG   CUT 2

C
F

HL

CL

FASH ON DESIGN

Hood Plan and Pattern

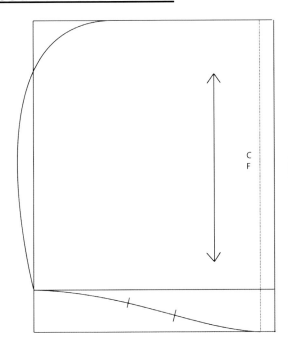

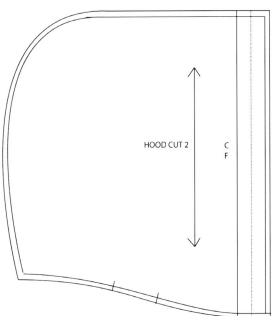

HOOD CUT 2

C F

13. CONTOURING

Contouring is to mould a garment to the body – fitting all the hollow areas and around the bust to create a perfect fit. The bust radius is 7.5cm (average size) a circle is drawn around the bust point with this radius. A total of 6 additional darts can be used to contour the front body (not all for one design) and 1 additional dart on the back bodice.

The additional dart at the centre front is to mould the bodice in between the bust.
The neckline and middle shoulder darts would be used for strapless styles.
Either of these additional darts can be used with the centre front dart.
The HPS shoulder and armhole dart are best used for shoulder (or off shoulder) styles.
The reduced shoulder darts would also be used for shoulder or off shoulder styles.

The additional dart from bust point to waistline can be also used for all styles.

Back bodice additional darts -
Waist dart extension would always be used.
Armhole dart would be used for sleeved styles.

The reduction at the side seam would also be used for all styles. This is actually a reduction of the ease in the block to ensure a very tight fit.

Contour Block

1. draw a line into the neckline – dart width is 6mm at radius, taper to neck
2. draw a line to the middle of the shoulder – dart width is 1.5cm at radius
3. draw a line to the shoulder point – dart width is 1.5cm at radius, taper to shoulder
4. draw a line to the notch point at the armhole – dart width is 6mm at armhole
5. extend the bust/ waist dart – 9mm width at radius, taper up to bust point and down to waistline.
6. draw a line out from the bust point to the centre front – dart is 9mm either side of the line
at centre front edge.
7. BACK bodice – dart to back armhole, 6mm width at armhole.
Extend back waist dart up to the cross back position.

The side seam is reduced up to 1.5cm at the top edge and 0.5cm at the waistline. For less fitted bustier reduce side seam at top edge by 1cm and taper to 0cm at waistline. Use the same measurement for the front and back. On the back panel the dart is extended to cross back, keeping dart width at the waistline the same.

Contour Block

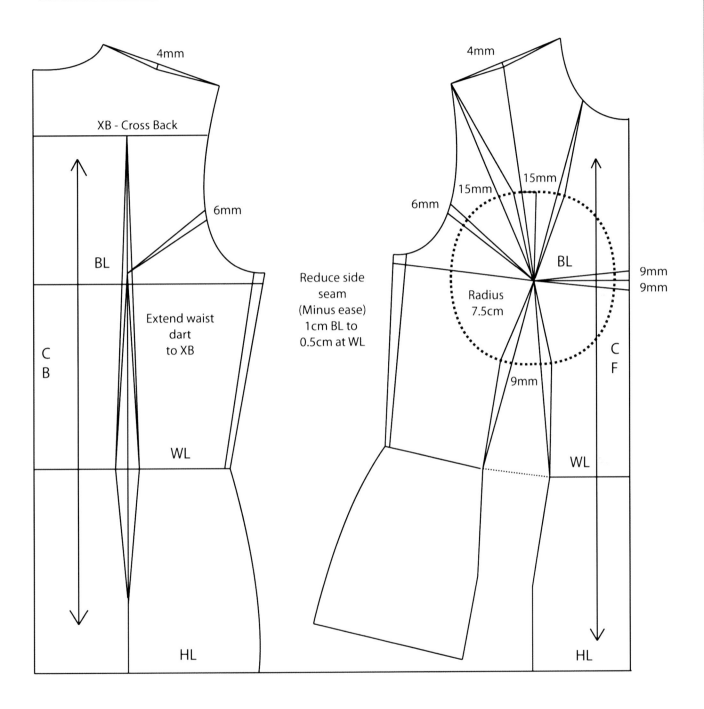

XB - Cross Back

4mm

6mm

BL

Extend waist
dart
to XB

C
B

WL

HL

Reduce side
seam
(Minus ease)
1cm BL to
0.5cm at WL

4mm

15mm

15mm

6mm

Radius
7.5cm

BL

9mm
9mm

9mm

C
F

WL

HL

FASHION DESIGN

Busier Without Cup - Plan A

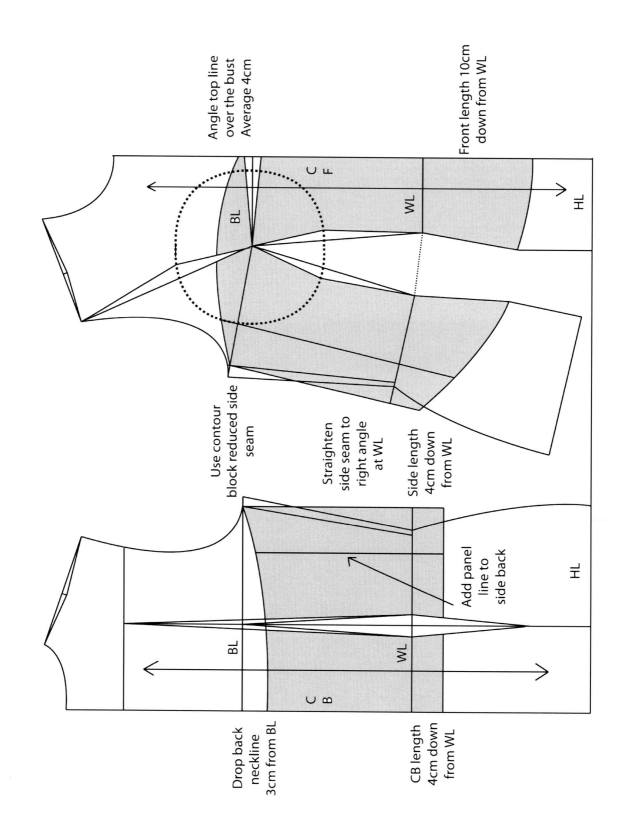

Angle top line
over the bust
Average 4cm

Front length 10cm
down from WL

Use contour
block reduced side
seam

Straighten
side seam to
right angle
at WL

Side length
4cm down
from WL

Add panel
line to
side back

Drop back
neckline
3cm from BL

CB length
4cm down
from WL

FASHION DESIGN

Busier Without Cup - Plan B

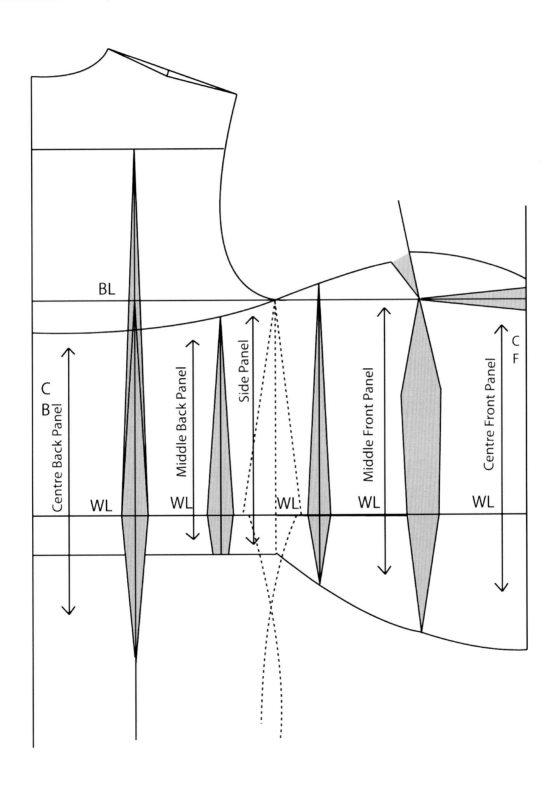

Centre Back Panel

CB

BL

WL

Middle Back Panel

WL

Side Panel

WL

Middle Front Panel

WL

Centre Front Panel

WL

CF

FASH ON DESIGN

Busier Without Cup - Pattern Pieces -

Without seam allowance as the different layers of a bustier have different seam allowances.

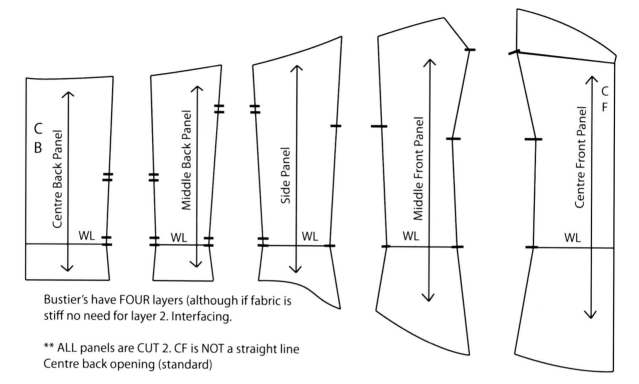

Bustier's have FOUR layers (although if fabric is stiff no need for layer 2. Interfacing.

** ALL panels are CUT 2. CF is NOT a straight line
Centre back opening (standard)

1. FABRIC = 1.3cm seam allowance
2. INTERFACING = 0.8cm seam allowance
3. CANVAS = 0.5cm seam allowance
4. LINING = 1cm seam allowance

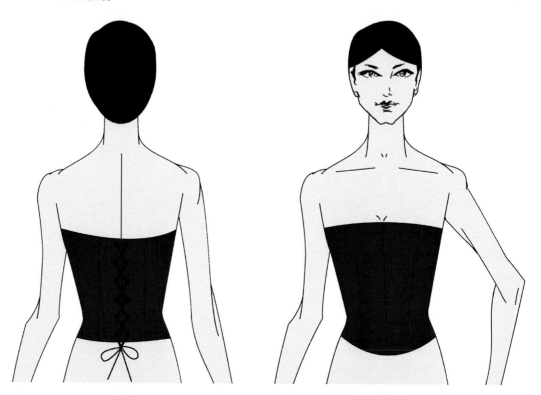

Bustier with Bust Cup Plan

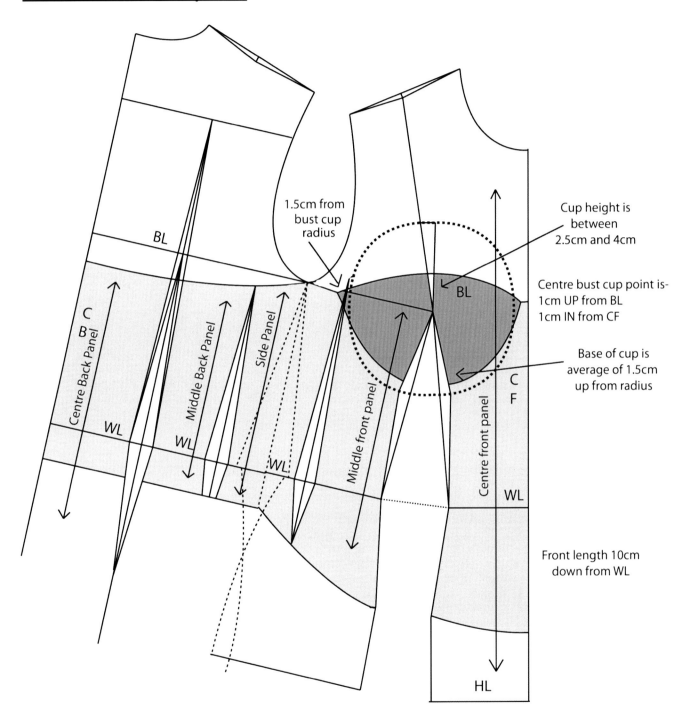

1.5cm from bust cup radius

Cup height is between 2.5cm and 4cm

Centre bust cup point is- 1cm UP from BL 1cm IN from CF

Base of cup is average of 1.5cm up from radius

Front length 10cm down from WL

BL

BL

C B

Centre Back Panel

Middle Back Panel

Side Panel

Middle front panel

Centre front panel

C F

WL

WL

WL

WL

WL

HL

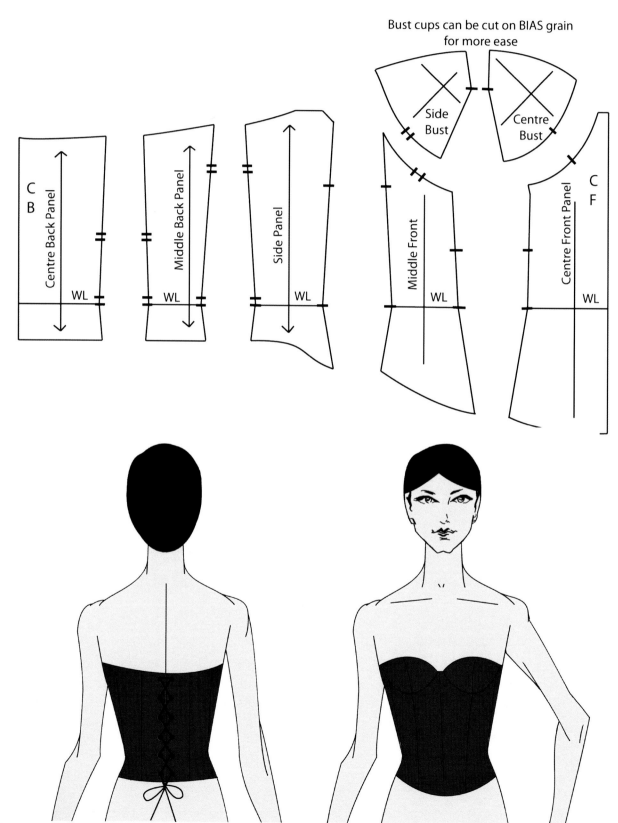

Bustier with Bust Cup Pattern Pieces -

Without seam allowance as the different layers of a bustier have different seam allowances.

Bust cups can be cut on BIAS grain for more ease

Side Bust

Centre Bust

C B

Centre Back Panel

WL

Middle Back Panel

WL

Side Panel

WL

Middle Front

WL

Centre Front Panel

C F

WL

Grading a Bust Cup

The bodice block creates an "A" bust cup. For a better silhouette it is advisable to grade to a "B" cup, using foam bust cups inside if required.

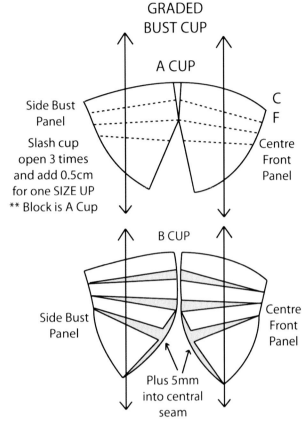

GRADED
BUST CUP

A CUP

Side Bust Panel

Slash cup open 3 times and add 0.5cm for one SIZE UP
** Block is A Cup

C F

Centre Front Panel

B CUP

Side Bust Panel

Centre Front Panel

Plus 5mm into central seam

** Grain lines can be cut on the BIAS for more ease over bust

Bustier Construction

Bustier's are made of four layers:-

1. Outer layer (chosen fabric) Add 1.3cm seam allowance to all seams. This allows the seam to "roll over" the edges and prevent the lining from being seen when the garment is worn.

2. Interfacing is the second layer. This is ironed onto the outer layer. Seam allowance is 0.8cm to ensure it is not touching the edge. Interfacing need not be used if the outer layer is a stiff firm fabric.

3. Canvas is the third layer. Also known as "horse hair". This has 0.5cm seam allowance – but no seam on the outside edges (just connecting seams). The horse hair is sewn flat – overlapping the 0.5cm seam allowance and sewing a line in the centre. This keeps the canvas flat.

4. Lining – seam allowance in 1cm.

FASH**I**ON
DESIGN

Bustier Sewing Instructions

1. Iron on interfacing to outer layer (if used)
2. Sew outer layer together – leaving open the closure (normally centre back)
3. Attach boning to each seam – DO NOT sew boning into the top and bottom edges seam allowance - start the boning under the seam allowance, and stop before the hem seam allowance. Boning options:-
a. Sew directly to the outer layer, stitch line should be through the seam
b. Sew a channel to the inside of the outer layer and insert the boning into it. This will give two 0.5cm seam lines either side of the seam on the outside
c. Sew boning through the 1.3cm seam allowance on the inside – this will give no stitch line on the outside but is the most unstable
4. Flat stitch the canvas layer together using the 0.5cm seam allowance
5. Hand stitch the canvas seam to the outer layer seams to fix together (canvas does not have seam allowance on the top and bottom edges so should cover the boning but not reach the edge.
6. Sew the lining together using 1cm seam allowance. LEAVE OPEN one of the longer seams. Catch this seam just 3cm at the top and 3cm at the bottom
7. Sew the lining to the top neck edge of the bustier
8. Turn inside and edge stitch 1mm on the lining – catching the seam allowance
9. Sew all remaining edges. The outer layer is slightly bigger than the lining, but once turned inside out and pressed it creates the "roll" and prevents the lining from being seen.
10. Turn bustier inside out using the lining open seam. Machine stitch the open lining seam together by folding in the seam allowance and stitching 1mm. Second option is to hand stitch this seam together.
11. Attach eyelets to centre back seam. Lace up.

** If a zipper is used best position is the side seam. Sew zipper on after step 6 then continue.

FASHION DESIGN

Bustier Sample Designs

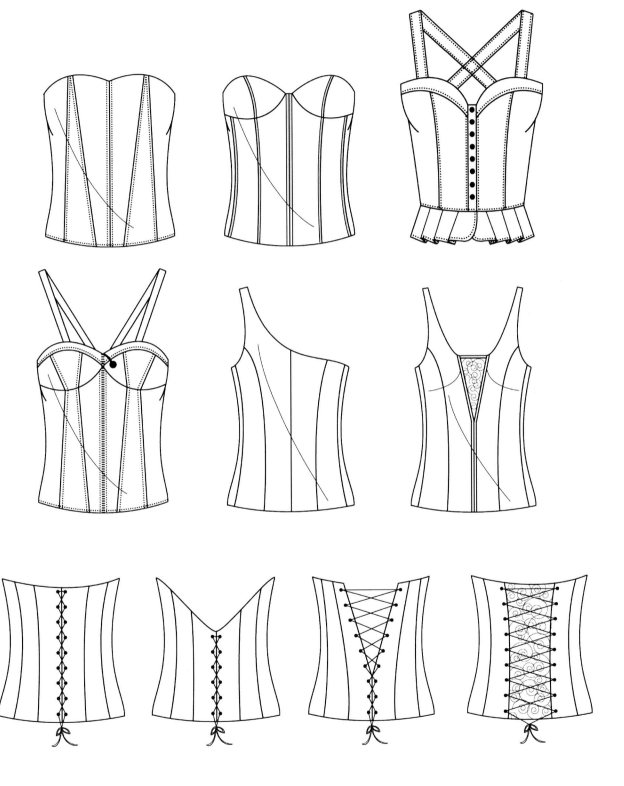

FASHION
DESIGN

14. TAILORING

The techniques of traditional tailoring are to use a more complicated pattern – from a 3 piece body block to a two piece sleeve to give a better shape over the arm. Tailored pockets are also fixed into the bodice and not stitched on top. The under construction of bespoke tailoring also used many hand techniques – hand basting canvas to the body instead of using interfacing, hand made shoulder pads and sleeve roll to give the shoulder line a better fit and nicer line.

Tailoring techniques are used in jackets and coats.

Over Garment Block

The over garment block can be used for tops, dresses, jackets and coats. It is a looser fitting block, combined with the over garment sleeve block. The armhole is lower, shoulder and body wider.

Bodice

Extend bodice at side seam by 1cm – BL, WL, HL
Drop armhole 2cm
Extend shoulder 0.5cm

Sleeve

1.   Lower sleeve head height by 1cm
2.   Add 2.5cm to Back sleeve width
3.   Add 2cm to Front sleeve width
4.   Re-draw Back sleeve head from notch to new lowered sleeve width line– matching the measurement with the bodice.
5.   Re-draw Front sleeve head from notch to new lowered sleeve width line– matching the measurement with the bodice.
6.   Increase elbow line by 1.5cm each side
7.   Increase cuff width by 1cm each side

FASHION DESIGN

Over Garment Block

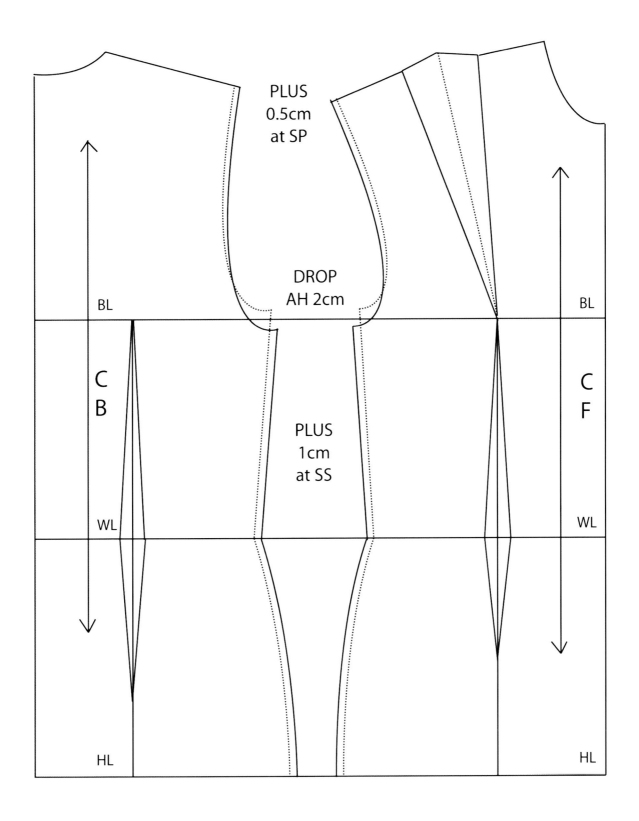

PLUS
0.5cm
at SP

DROP
AH 2cm

PLUS
1cm
at SS

BL

BL

C
B

C
F

WL

WL

HL

HL

FASHION DESIGN

Over Garment Sleeve Block

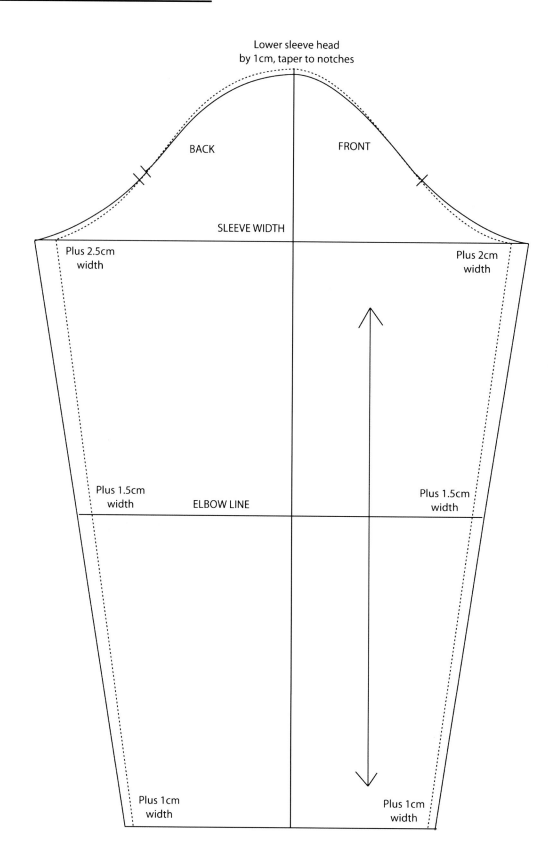

Lower sleeve head
by 1cm, taper to notches

BACK   FRONT

SLEEVE WIDTH

Plus 2.5cm
width

Plus 2cm
width

Plus 1.5cm
width

ELBOW LINE

Plus 1.5cm
width

Plus 1cm
width

Plus 1cm
width

Tailored Jacket Block

A tailored jacket has an additional side panel, which is created by taking some away from the back bodice and some from the front bodice. The waist shaping is moved into the new side panel seams to give distributed shaping around the body. It is a more expensive block due to the additional seams but fits the body better as the ease is distributed better around the 3D body form.

The tailored jacket block can be used with either the over garment sleeve block or the two piece sleeve block. The two piece sleeve block also gives better shaping over the arm as the seams are shaped.

To construct the Tailored Jacket Block - use over garment block

1.   Trace block keeping WL, HL in line. Place HL at SS point together.
2.   Draw a central line up to SP
3.   Move Back dart to CB seam – minus 3cm at WL, minus 1cm HL, taper UP to XB
4.   Draw a new line for the Back side panel seam – 7cm along WL from SS
5.   Square down to HL, mark a point at 14cm below WL
6.   Square up to BL then curve outwards to 2.5cm below XB
7.   Draw a new line for the Front side panel seam – 2cm along from WL
8.   Square down to HL, mark a point at 14cm below WL
9.   Square up to 0.5cm under BL (keeping 2cm from SS)
10.   Move the back waistline excess into the back seam, creating a 3cm dart (1.5cm either side of seam line) Taper down to 14cm under WL. Taper up to BL
11.   Move front waistline excess into front side panel seam, 1.5cm each side of seam line. Taper down to 14cm below WL, taper up to armhole
12.   Trace off new side seam panel – there is 3.5cm excess at BL (due to bust being smaller than hip). Slash down the original side line (extension UP from SS HL) slash along WL on side panel and overlap at top edge the 3.5cm excess. This will cause a 0.5cm overlap at the WL

FASH**ON DESIGN

Tailored Jacket Block Construction

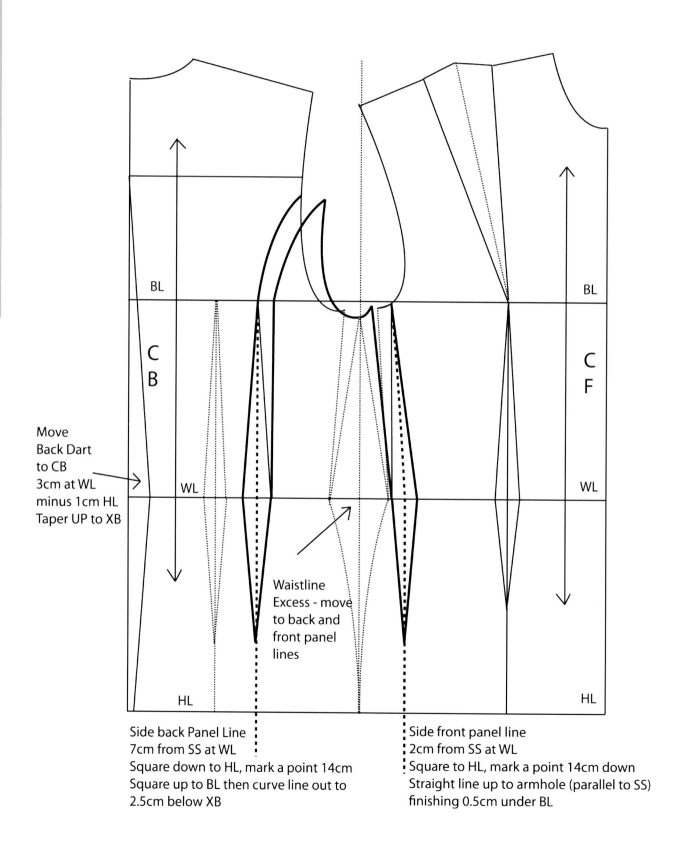

BL

C
B

Move
Back Dart
to CB
3cm at WL
minus 1cm HL
Taper UP to XB

WL

Waistline
Excess - move
to back and
front panel
lines

HL

Side back Panel Line
7cm from SS at WL
Square down to HL, mark a point 14cm
Square up to BL then curve line out to
2.5cm below XB

BL

C
F

WL

HL

Side front panel line
2cm from SS at WL
Square to HL, mark a point 14cm down
Straight line up to armhole (parallel to SS)
finishing 0.5cm under BL

Tailored Jacket Block Plan

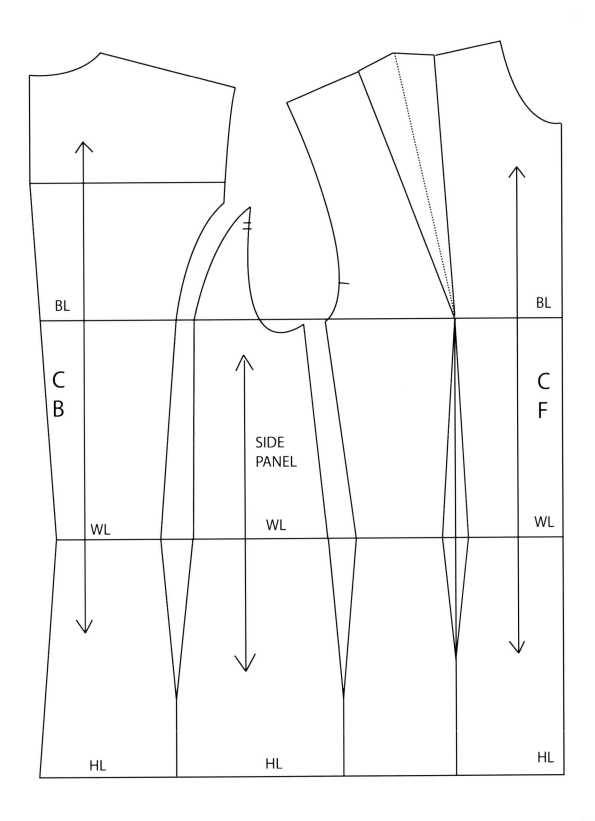

Two Piece Sleeve Block - Use over garment sleeve block

1. Trace sleeve block. Mark a point 6cm from hemline at Back, 8cm at Elbow line. Draw line from sleeve hem to armhole curve
2. Trace off a 5cm parallel line from the Front sleeve and matching side seam place at the back of the sleeve
3. Reduce front top sleeve line by 3cm at Elbow. Taper UP with a curve and down to hem line with a straight line.
4. MIRROR image the under sleeve and place inside top sleeve – aligning elbow line.
5. Increase back sleeve seam by 2cm at Elbow line. Curve up to armhole line, down to hemline
6. Under sleeve front seam – curve in 2cm at Elbow line, taper up with a curve and down to hemline
7. Drop underarm hole side seam point by 0.5cm, join with a smooth curve
8. Increase back sleeve seam by 2cm at hemline – connect with front sleeve seam

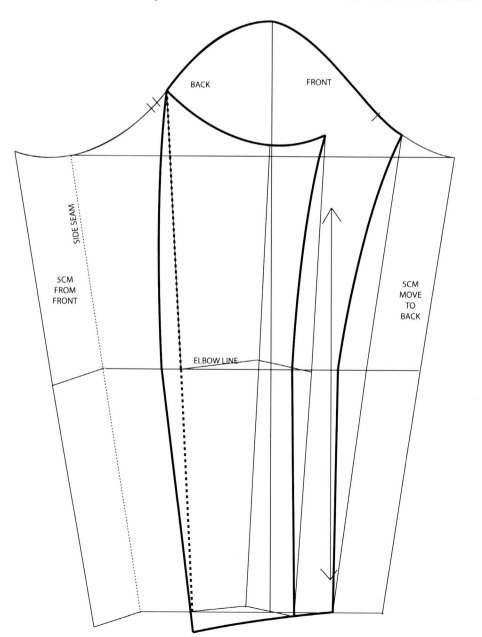

FASHION DESIGN

Two Piece Sleeve Plan

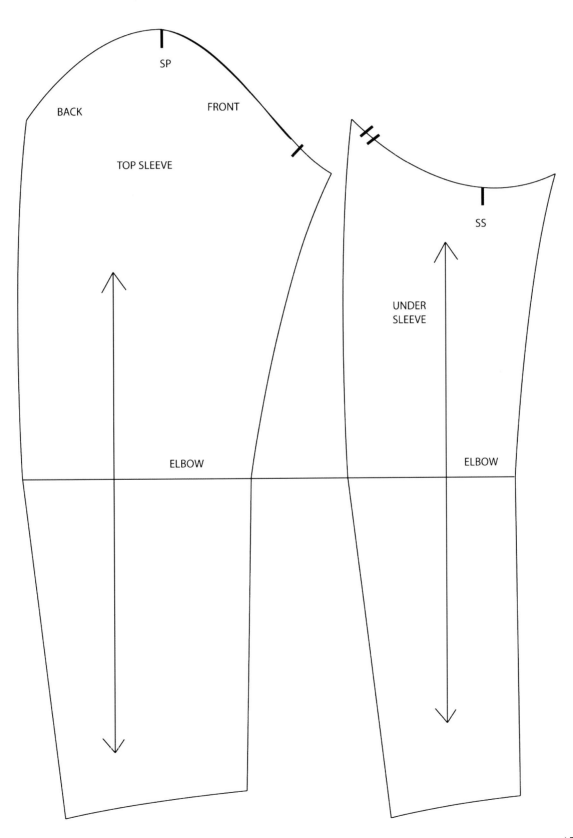

FASHON DESIGN

Tailored Jacket Sample Design

Single Breasted Tailored Jacket

Double Breasted Tailored Jacket

FASHION DESIGN

Button Sizes

Buttons are measured in "LINE". Below is a guide to show what line equates to in millimeters.

LINE	MM's	
30	19	
28	17.5	
26	16.5	
25	15	
24	14	
20	12.5	
18	11	
16	10	
14	8.5	

LINE	MM's	
54	34	
46	28	
40	25	
36	22.5	
34	21.5	
32	20	

Bespoke Tailoring Techniques

Hand basting canvas

Instead of using iron on interfacing canvas (also known as horse hair) can be hand stitched to the front and side panels. It is stitched within seam allowance with a basting stitch just to fix together.

Break Line tape

Break line tape – which is 1cm interfacing strips is hand stitched to the break line on the rever. The rever needs to be "rolled" over fore finger to fix the shape. Two rows of small basting stitches in a diagonal position are stitched along the edges. You need to catch the canvas and outer body without showing the stitches on the outside.

Shoulder Pads

Hand made shoulder pads give the exact height and shape required for tailored jackets. The shoulder pad is made by layers of felt and one layer of canvas. The length of the shoulder pad runs from the XF to XB position. Width is shoulder minus 1cm. Create the outside layers of the shoulder pad (2 pieces in felt) then create smaller layers for the inside – reducing 2cm in length and width. The smallest layer should be 8cm length x 6cm width and made in canvas. The key thing to remember is to create a gradation in size by using different sizes of pad inside. Stitch by hand the shoulder pad onto the seam of the shoulder. Catch the shoulder pad along the shoulder seam at the neck point.

Sleeve Roll

Sleeve roll is used on the shoulder head to give a nice finish to the shoulder line where the sleeve "rolls" over the arm. This is constructed with felt and an inside layer of canvas. The felt is 6cm wide. Canvas 3cm wide. Fold the canvas inside the felt and hand stitch to fix – showing 1cm below canvas. Length is the same as the shoulder pad length.

Under Collar

A tailored under collar is cut 2 on the bias grain. Canvas is cut 2 without CB seam. Hand stitch canvas to under collar – then construct collar with outer collar layer before fixing to tailored jacket. Traditionally the under collar is made of a wool called Melton, which is a type of felted wool. This quality molds well and gives a perfect collar finish.

FASHION DESIGN

Tailor Made Shoulder Pads

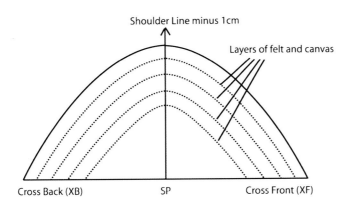

Shoulder Line minus 1cm

Layers of felt and canvas

Cross Back (XB)   SP   Cross Front (XF)

Front View of Shoulder Pad with sleeve roll on the right side

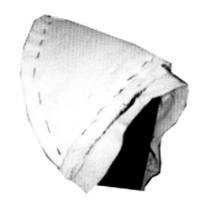

Side View of Shoulder Pad Showing sleeve roll which would sit on the sleeve head, inside the garment

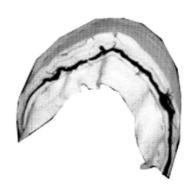

Sleeve Roll

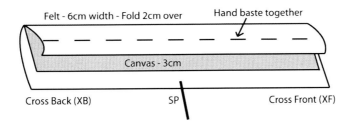

Felt - 6cm width - Fold 2cm over   Hand baste together

Canvas - 3cm

Cross Back (XB)   SP   Cross Front (XF)

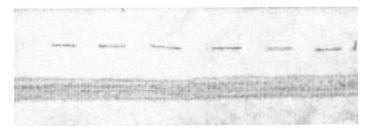

15. POCKETS

Pockets can be placed anywhere on garments. Most are functional – for hands or wallets and credit cards. There are three predominant pocket styles

1. Patch Pockets – an additional pattern piece applied onto the main garment

2. Pockets in side seams – where part of the bodice is cut away for the pocket to be constructed

3. Tailored pockets – where the pocket is constructed within the bodice block.

Patch pockets

Patch pockets are generally found on casual wear garments. The back of jeans, the inside of a jeans front side seam pocket also has a small patch pocket. This style of pocket can be any size, design and placed anywhere. Patch pockets can be just a design detail or functional.

For pattern construction drill holes need to be placed on pattern and plan for the placement of the patch pockets. The drill holes mark the position of the patch pocket to make sewing the garment easier.

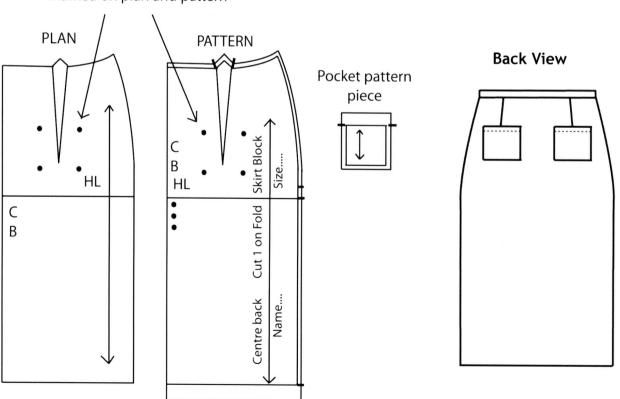

FASHION DESIGN

Patch Pocket Sample Designs

PLEATED POCKETS

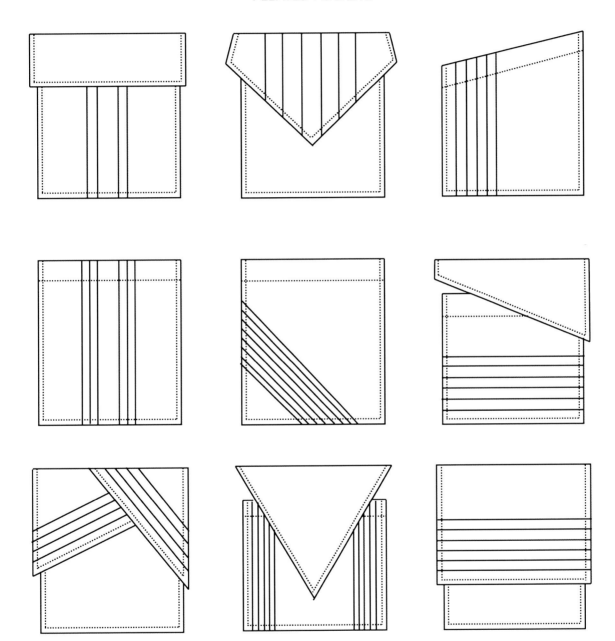

FASHION DESIGN

Patch Pocket Sample Designs

POCKETS WITH TABS

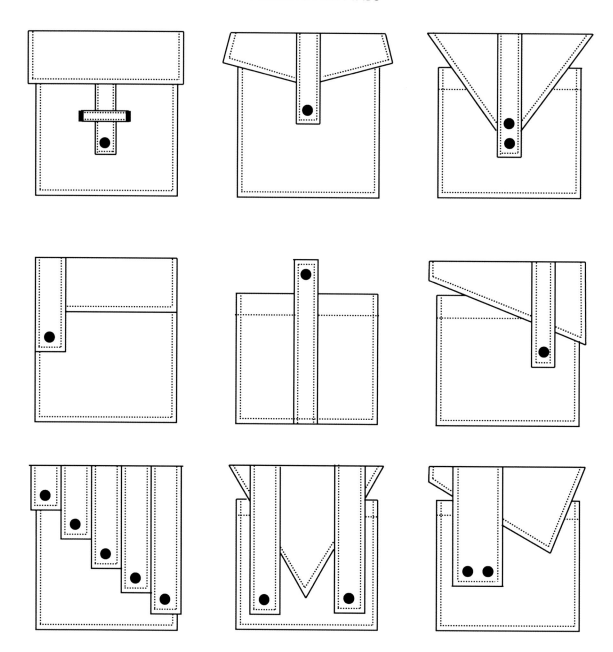

FASHION DESIGN

3D Patch Pocket Sample Designs

To create a 3D pocket a rectangular panel needs to be added to enable the pocket to be raised away from the garment. This panel is the total side length of the pocket – width is optional – average of 4cm. The panel is sewn firstly the patch pocket, and secondly to the garment. The actual pocket is not sewn to the garment. The rectangle panel added to create the 3D pocket can be smaller at the top opening edges to have less 3D effect at the top.

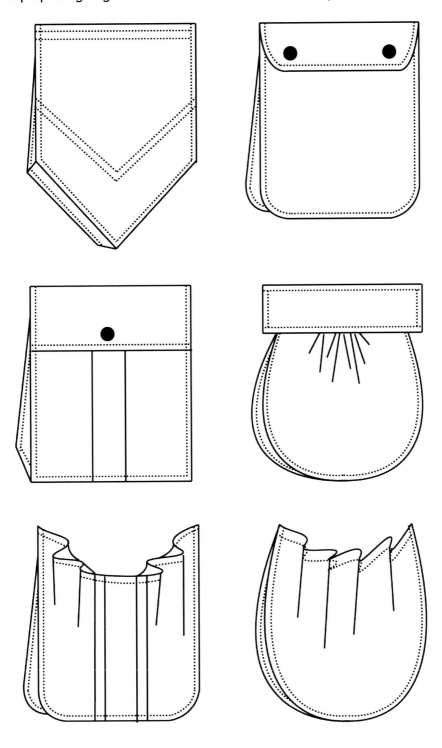

Pockets in Side Seam

Many pockets are placed in a side seam on trousers and skirts. The pocket opening seam is the style line. It can be high and round as seen on many jeans styles, or slim and long as seen on tailored men's trousers. Pockets in side seams have the front panel reduced to accomodate the pocket, a pocket lining which also has the reduced side edge, and a pocket back made of the actual fabric which is the original side seam. The pocket back is what is seen behind the pocket opening.

The front panel of trousers or skirts is shaped with the pocket style line (the opening)
Pocket bag size would be big enough for your hand or wallet. Some pockets are big inside, others smaller. An average size would be down to the hipline and across 10cm from side seam.

The pocket back size is the original side seam line across to the pocket bag depth and width. The pocket lining is the new shaped front edge

The pocket back and pocket lining can be cut as one piece, joining at the base, but then a facing is required to cover the pocket opening. This method is common in jeans where the lining is made of a fine cotton.

POCKETS IN SIDE SEAM

Front View

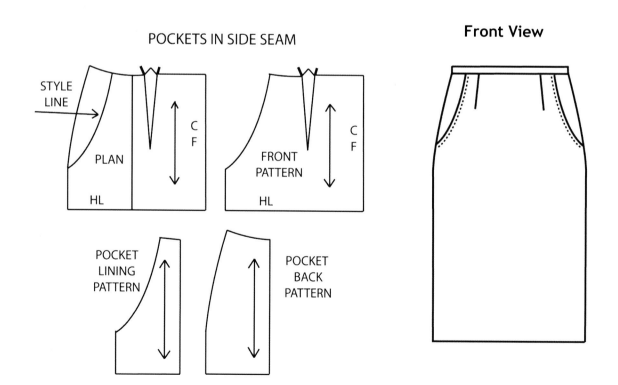

FASH ON DESIGN

Side Seam Pocket Sample Designs

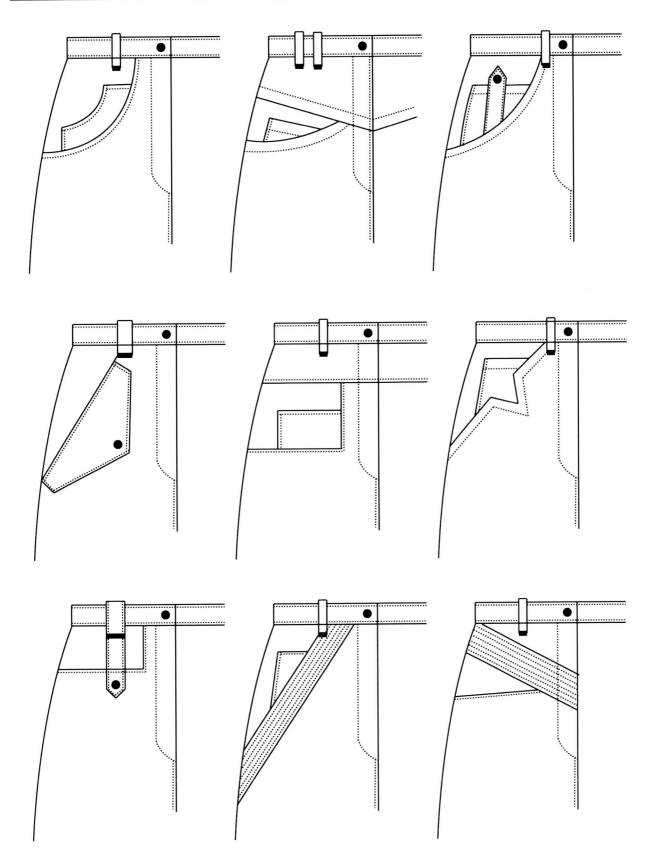

Tailored Pockets

Tailored pockets are cut out from the garment. There are two types of tailored pockets. Welt pockets which are made of a rectangle folded at the top for the opening. Jet pockets are two small strips of fabric folded over to create a small slit opening. Jet pockets can also be made with flaps attached to the top edge. A pocket bag pattern needs to be made for the inside of the pocket which is attached to the opening only and left to "hang" inside. Drill holes must be placed on the plan and pattern for pocket placement.

Welt Pocket

Welt pockets are commonly seen at the top breast point of coats and jackets. They are generally small, the size of a wallet or credit card. Welt pockets can be longer and used as main pockets also.

A line is marked on the plan for the placement and length of the welt.
The welt pattern is double the width of the finished size with the folded edge at the top. The sides of the welt may not be a right angle if the pocket position is at an angle.
The lining pattern is also on the fold at the bottom edge. The lining can also have a facing at the top but this is not necessary as the inside of the welt cannot be seen when worn. The lining width is 1cm longer each side of the welt.

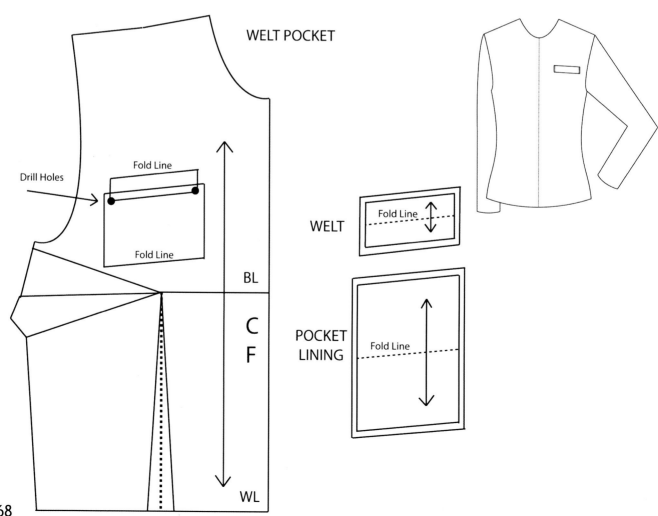

Jet Pocket

A jet pocket is made from two strips of fabric being attached to the bodice to create a "slit" style of pocket. The widths of these strips are an average of 1cm. The pattern is 4cm width to allow for the folded top edge and seam allowance of 1cm each side. The pocket lining would be cut on fold at the bottom edge and made with a facing as when the pocket is used the inside of the back of the lining is visible. The lining length is determined by the length of the jacket and the use of the pocket. An average would be 15cm. The best position for a jet pocket is 6cm under the waistline.

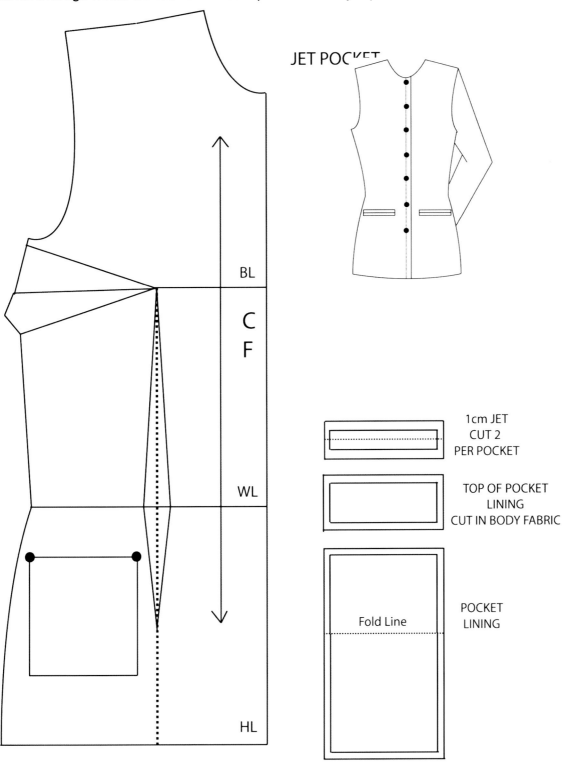

JET POCKET

BL

C
F

WL

HL

1cm JET
CUT 2
PER POCKET

TOP OF POCKET
LINING
CUT IN BODY FABRIC

Fold Line

POCKET
LINING

FASHION DESIGN

Jet Pocket with Flap

A jet and flap pocket is where an additional flap is added to the top jet. This flap is a rectangle, cut on the fold at the bottom edge. The flap hides the bottom jet pocket. The pocket flap can be any width, but is the same length as the jet pocket.

The jet flap would be the same length as the jets. Cut on fold at the bottom edge
Jet is 4cm total width for the pattern pieces including seam allowance.
Lining can also have a facing although the flap will partially hide the lining when the pocket is used.

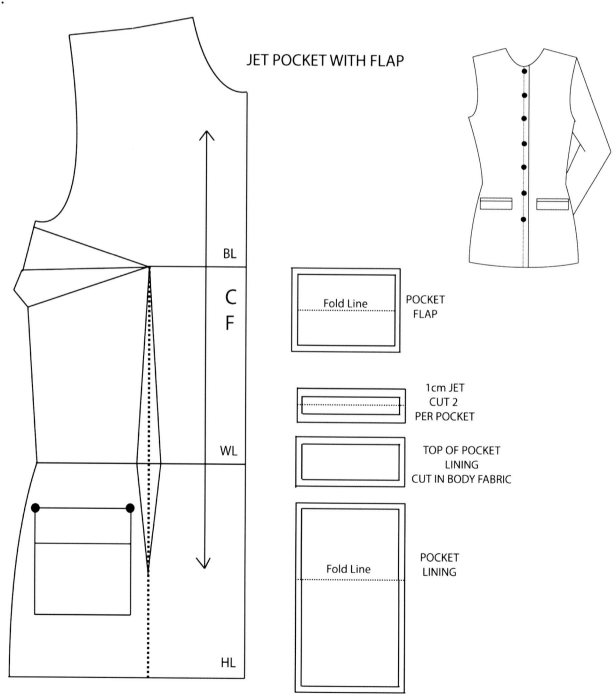

JET POCKET WITH FLAP

POCKET FLAP

Fold Line

1cm JET
CUT 2
PER POCKET

TOP OF POCKET
LINING
CUT IN BODY FABRIC

POCKET
LINING

Fold Line

BL

C
F

WL

HL

FASHION DESIGN

Jet Pocket Construction

OUTSIDE OF GARMENT

STEP 1

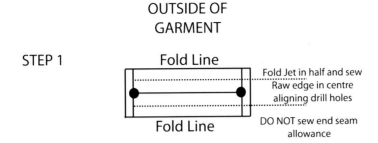

Fold Line

Fold Line

Fold Jet in half and sew
Raw edge in centre
aligning drill holes

DO NOT sew end seam
allowance

INSIDE OF GARMENT

STEP 2

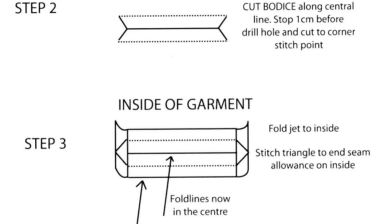

CUT BODICE along central
line. Stop 1cm before
drill hole and cut to corner
stitch point

INSIDE OF GARMENT

STEP 3

Fold jet to inside

Stitch triangle to end seam
allowance on inside

Foldlines now
in the centre

Raw edge now on outside

STEP 4

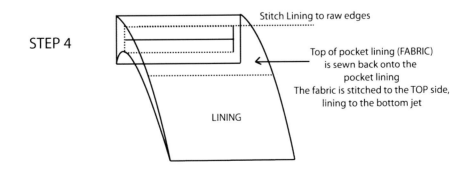

Stitch Lining to raw edges

Top of pocket lining (FABRIC)
is sewn back onto the
pocket lining
The fabric is stitched to the TOP side,
lining to the bottom jet

LINING

STEP 5 - Sew sides of lining

16. COATS

Coats can be constructed using either the over garment block or the tailored jacket block depending on the design.

Sample shown is made from the tailored jacket block, with a rever collar and jet and flap pockets. It also has a 4cm back open vent, which is traditionally used with tailored coats. There is a 4cm hem on the pattern, which is also typical for tailored coats. Some tailored coats also have vents on the sleeves but these tend to be closed vents with buttons attached over the top. Back vents can also be in the back to side panel, where the coat would have two vents. This is also seen on tailored jackets.

The lining pattern is best constructed using the least amount of seams possible as it has the most stress when worn. The lining would be cut on fold at CB and a rectangle cut out for making the open vent. Only 1cm hem is added onto lining, then fixed to the hemline of the outer body. This gives a 2cm overlap of lining at the hemlines, which allow for movement. The same is done for the sleeve lining.

Vent Openings

Vents are generally seen on the back of coats, jackets and on sleeves. Open vents are on the back, closed vents on sleeve cuffs. Vents can be placed into the side panel seam at the back or the centre back. Open vents would work on any open seam, even sleeves. Closed vents have buttons sewn over the top on the sleeve of tailored jackets.

A back vent can also be constructed by using the inverted box pleat. Even having a button opening closure in the inside.

Open Vents

Open vents have a different pattern piece as one side is folded back at the CB seam (or chosen seam for the vent placement). The other side has an extension of the same width, which comes out from the CB seam, topstitched all together at the top of the vent. If there was no extension it would be a split and not a vent.

Closed Vents

Closed vents have the same pattern piece as the vent is an extension from the CB seam. The edges are then stitched together, and topstitched through to the right side.

FASHION DESIGN

OPEN VENT

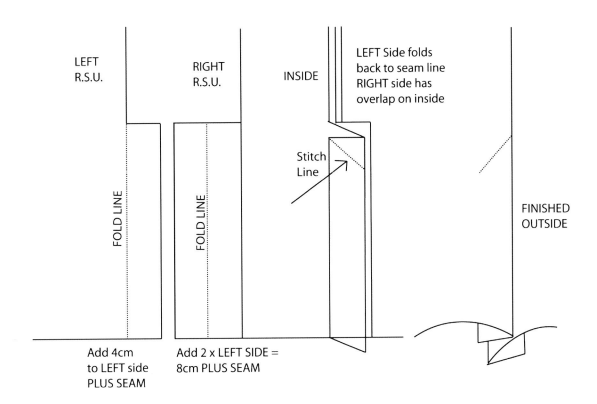

LEFT R.S.U.

RIGHT R.S.U.

INSIDE

LEFT Side folds back to seam line RIGHT side has overlap on inside

FOLD LINE

FOLD LINE

Stitch Line

FINISHED OUTSIDE

Add 4cm to LEFT side PLUS SEAM

Add 2 x LEFT SIDE = 8cm PLUS SEAM

CLOSED VENT

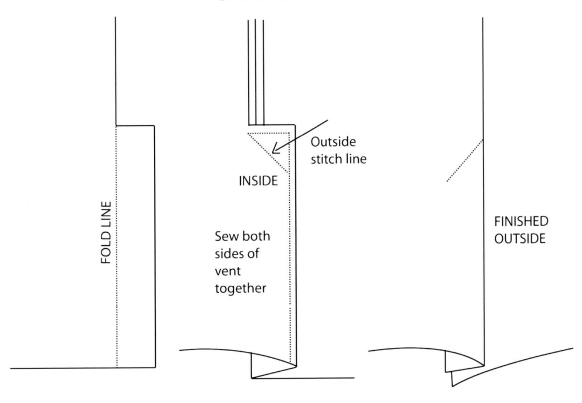

FOLD LINE

Outside stitch line

INSIDE

Sew both sides of vent together

FINISHED OUTSIDE

Tailored Coat Design - Plan

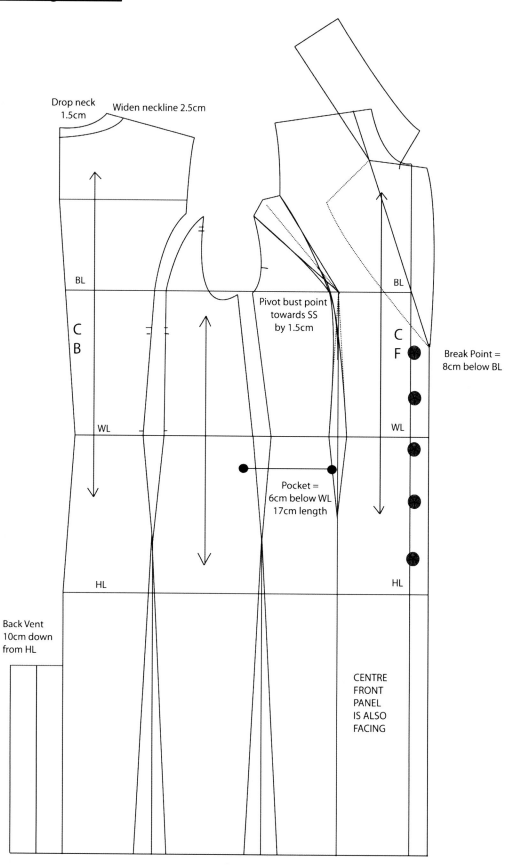

Drop neck
1.5cm

Widen neckline 2.5cm

BL

C
B

WL

HL

Back Vent
10cm down
from HL

Pivot bust point
towards SS
by 1.5cm

Pocket =
6cm below WL
17cm length

BL

C
F

Break Point =
8cm below BL

WL

HL

CENTRE
FRONT
PANEL
IS ALSO
FACING

Plus 2cm at hem of side panel seams
taper to dart

3cm Button
Stand

FASHION DESIGN

Tailored Coat - Back and Side Panel Pattern
1cm seam allowance and 4cm hem allowance

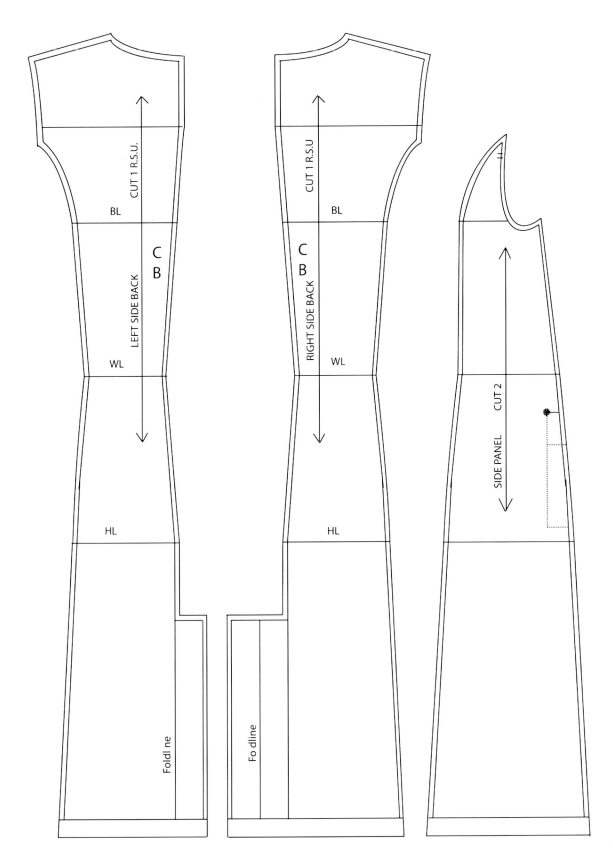

FASH*ON DESIGN

Tailored Coat - Front, pocket and collar Pattern

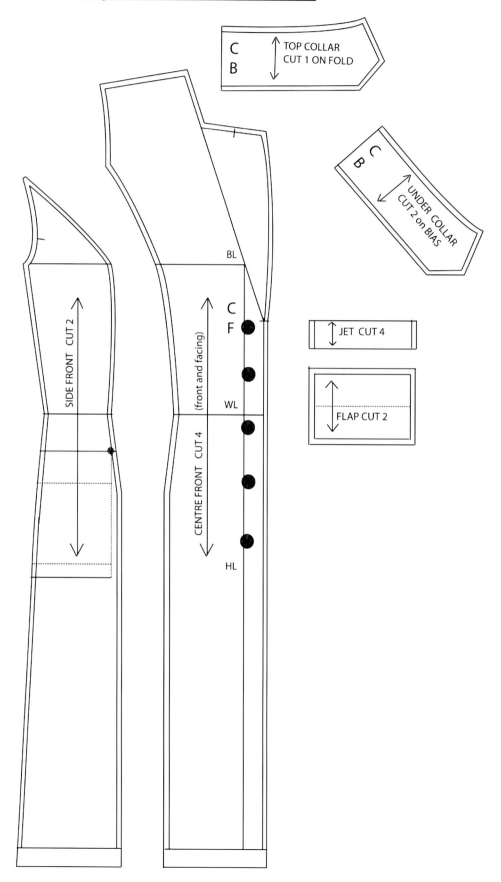

C
B
↕ TOP COLLAR
CUT 1 ON FOLD

C
B
UNDER COLLAR
CUT 2 on BIAS

SIDE FRONT CUT 2

BL

C
F

(front and facing)

WL

CENTRE FRONT   CUT 4

HL

JET CUT 4

FLAP CUT 2

FASH┇ON DESIGN

Two piece Sleeve Plan

Pattern
Add 1cm seam allowance and 4cm hem allowance (same as tailored coat body panels)

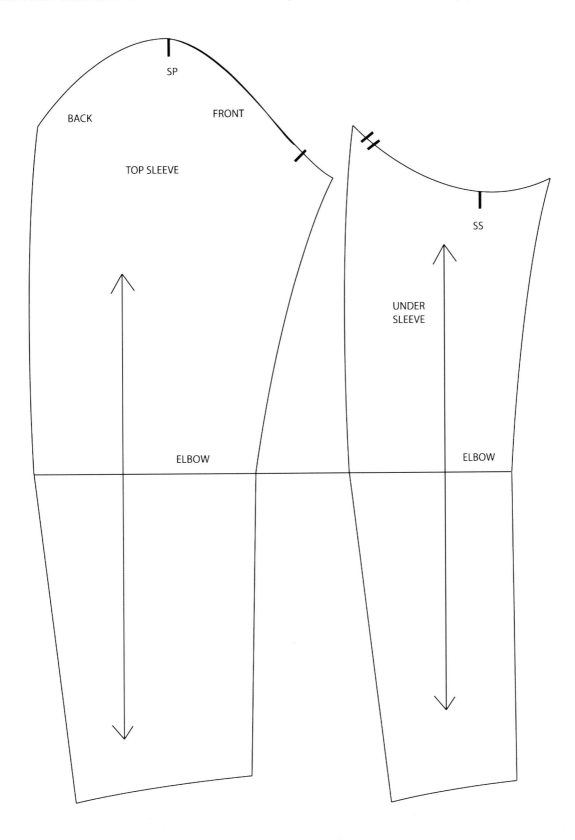

Coat Lining Pattern

Back panel is cut one Right Side Up, with a cut out rectangle for the back open vent. The lining is larger at the waistline for ease of movement when the coat is worn. The sleeve lining is the same pattern pieces as the outer body apart from the hem being just 1cm.

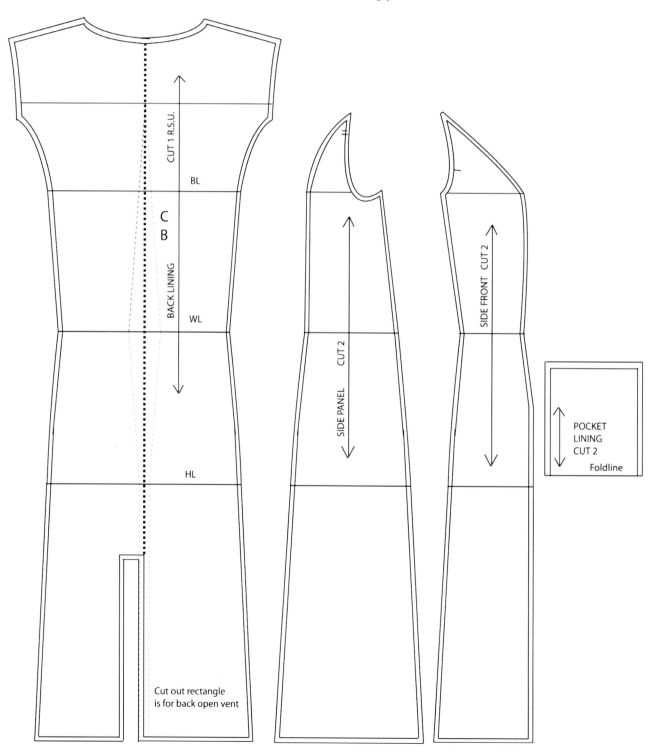

FASHION DESIGN

Tailored Coat Sample Design

FASHON DESIGN

Tailored Coat Sample Design

FASHION DESIGN

17. JERSEY GARMENTS

Jersey Garment Information

Jersey garments are made from specific blocks that have no body darts. There are also specific types of machinery used for making jersey garments. The traditional sewing machine is called a "lock stitch" and this is not suitable for sewing jersey fabric as it does not allow the jersey to stretch when worn, and the stitches will easily break. Seams on jersey garments are overlocked with a 5 thread overlocker. Finishing necklines is predominantly done with a binding machine, another specialized machine which sews binding from 0.5cm up to around 6cm wide. Hem's on jersey garments are finished with a twin needle machine – where two lines of thread are seen on the outside and an overlocking stitch on the inside – this type of stitch also has natural stretch. Some less stretch jersey fabrics can be sewn with a lock stitch machine but care must be taken not to rip the stitches open when the garment is worn.

Typical jersey garments are t-shirts, polo shirts, camisoles, vests etc. A common jersey is 95% cotton and 5% lycra. There are now many types of man made jersey fabrics used in all garment classifications, from heavy to light weight. Most jersey fabrics have a good drape.

** The guide below is for limited stretch fabrics. For maximum stretch reduce BL, WL, HL up to 12cm total.

** Jersey blocks have NO EASE as they are made to fit the body tightly.

Measurement	Original SIZE 10 Measurement	Jersey Measurement
BL – Bust Line	83cm	Minus 4cm
WL – Waist Line	67cm	Minus 4cm
HL – Hip Line	90cm	Minus 8cm
CBL - Nape to waist	43cm	Same
Shoulder	12cm	Minus 2cm
Shoulder lope		2.5cm
Armhole Depth	20cm	Minus 2cm
XB – Cross Back	33.5cm	Minus 3.5cm
Neck opening width	7cm	Minus 1cm
Back neck drop	2cm	Minus 1cm
Front neck drop	8cm	Minus 1cm
Body Rise	27cm	Same
WL to floor	100cm	Same
Sleeve length	58cm	Same
Sleeve head height	14cm	10cm
Wrist	15.5cm	Same
Knee	32cm	
Ankle	20.4cm	

FASH♀ON DESIGN

Jersey Bodice Block

The jersey bodice block would be used to make tops and dresses. It is a very fitted block so works best on all fitted designs. For loose fitting jersey garments like cardigan and jacket styles the over garment block is best used.

Bodice

1.   Trace back bodice block
2.   Reduce HL to 20.5cm
3.   Reduce WL to 15.75cm
4.   Reduce BL to 19.75cm
5.   Connect new side seam
6.   Measure CBL from WL UP to neck point mark 43cm
7.   Reduce neck opening by 1cm.
8.   Back neck drop = 1cm
9.   Front neck drop = 7cm
10.   Draw new shoulder line 10cm length – (dropped by 1.5cm)
11.   Connect a line from SP to SS 18cm in length
12.   Shape new armhole
13.   Back dart NOT USED

Sleeve

1.   Draw central line 58cm length
2.   Mark shoulder height line at 10cm from HPS
3.   Draw a straight line from HPS to shoulder width line – the measurement of the curved armhole = 20cm
4.   Mark a mid way point down the line.
5.   Curve line UP 1.5cm, and reduce by 0.5cm
6.   Mark elbow line at 35cm down from HPS.
7.   Elbow width = 24cm. mark a point at 12cm
8.   Wrist = 18cm, mark a point at 9cm
9.   Connect side seam of sleeve

![Fashion Design header]

FASHION DESIGN

Jersey Bodice Block

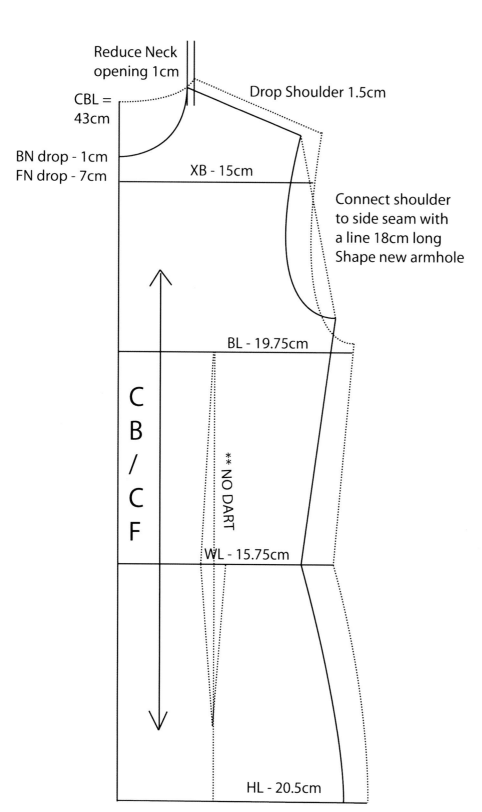

Reduce Neck opening 1cm

Drop Shoulder 1.5cm

CBL = 43cm

BN drop - 1cm
FN drop - 7cm

XB - 15cm

Connect shoulder to side seam with a line 18cm long
Shape new armhole

BL - 19.75cm

C
B
/
C
F

** NO DART

WL - 15.75cm

HL - 20.5cm

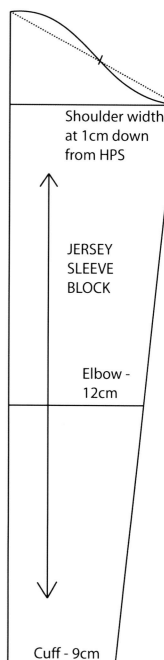

Shoulder width at 1cm down from HPS

JERSEY SLEEVE BLOCK

Elbow - 12cm

Cuff - 9cm

Jersey Top Sample Designs

FASHION DESIGN

Jersey Dress Sample Designs

Jersey Cardigan/ Jacket Sample Designs

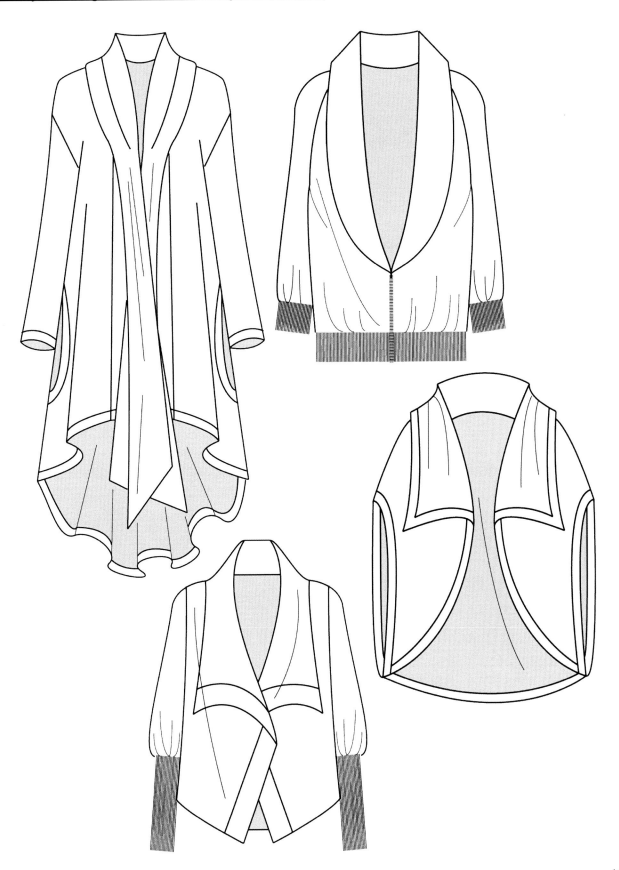

187

Jersey Leggings Block

1. Trace FRONT trouser block
2. Raise CL by 1cm
3. Mark HL measurement = 20.5cm (HL – 8cm – EASE on block)
4. Square UP to WL and DOWN to Hem Line
5. Reduce CF seam by 1cm – taper to HL
6. Reduce CB seam by 4cm – raise by 3cm – taper to HL
7. Connect new CB line with SS line with a curve
8. Front CL extension = 2.5cm – create a smooth curve and taper to HL
9. Back CL extension = 4cm – create a smooth curve and taper to HL
10. Reduce knee line at inside leg – FRONT = 16cm, BACK = 17cm
11. Reduce Ankle at inside leg – FRONT = 12cm, BACK = 13cm
12. Mirror image back leg from SS to create leggings bloc

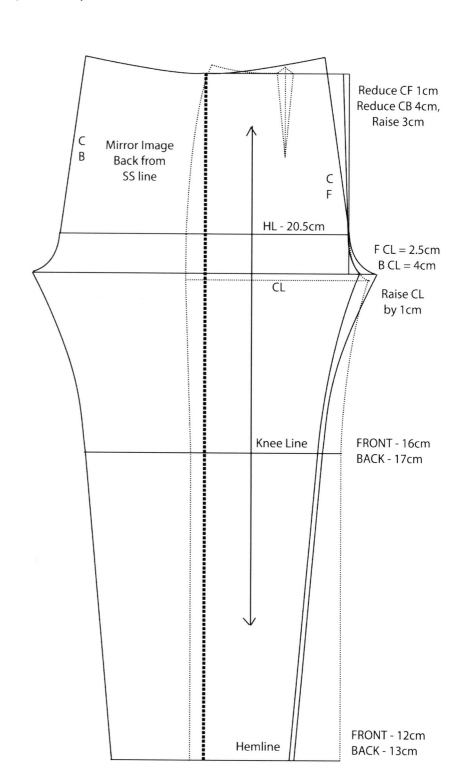

C B

Mirror Image Back from SS line

Reduce CF 1cm
Reduce CB 4cm,
Raise 3cm

C F

HL - 20.5cm

F CL = 2.5cm
B CL = 4cm

CL

Raise CL by 1cm

Knee Line

FRONT - 16cm
BACK - 17cm

Hemline

FRONT - 12cm
BACK - 13cm

FASHION

Jersey Leggings Sample Designs

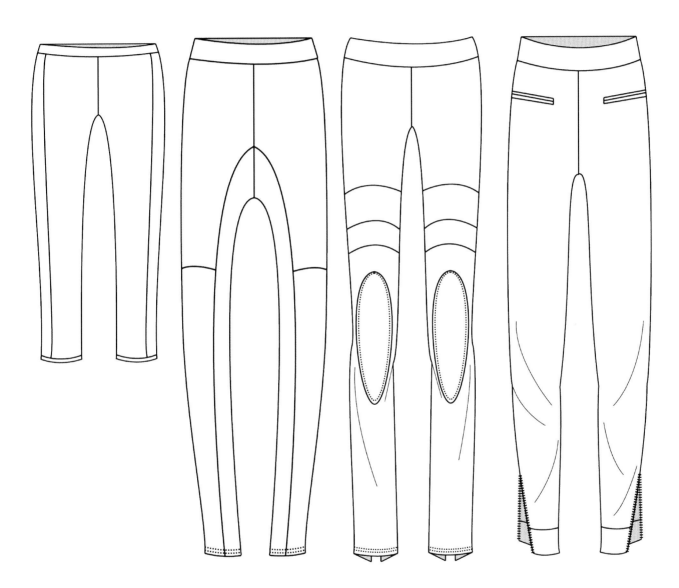

18. GRADING

Grading is the term used to change patterns to bigger or smaller sizes. The standard grade between two sizes is 5cm at the bust, waist and hipline. Grading works best for up or down 3 sizes only as our body shapes change in different ways for much larger or smaller sizes. It is therefore advisable to create new blocks from measurements of the larger or smaller sizes.

Measurement	10	Grade
BL - Bust line - approx 24cm down from H.P.S.	83	5cm
WL - Waist line - 41cm down from centre back neck	67	5cm
HL - Hip line - Low hip is 20cm down from WL	90	5cm
CBL - centre back length - from centre back neck	43	0.6cm
Waist to floor length	100	1cm
Waist to knee	55	0.5cm
S - shoulder - total measurement	40	1.2cm
Shoulder - one side	12	0.3cm
Neck size	35.6	1.5cm
XB - Back width - measure 11cm down from BC Neck	33.5	1.2cm
XF - Chest - measure 12cm down from H.P.S	31	1.2cm
Bust dart width	6	0.6cm
Bust dart length at side seam position	10	0.9cm
Front waist dart width	3	0cm
Front waist dart length - WL to finish	10	0cm
Back waist dart width	3	0cm
Back waist dart length - WL to finish	14	0cm
Back neck opening - fitted neckline	14	0.6cm
Front neck drop - measure from H.P.S.	8	0.2cm
Armhole depth	20	0.3cm
BR - Body rise - from WL	27	0.7cm
Knee	32	1.6cm
Ankle	20.4	0.6cm
Sleeve length	58	0.5cm
Bicep - measure 2.5cm down from armhole	26.4	1.6cm
Elbow	22	1cm
Wrist	15.5	0.5cm

Pivot Grading

There are different methods of grading used including computer grading. Pivot grading is a method where you move "pivot" the original block around the page to create the next size – either one size bigger or one size smaller. Start from the Centre front or centre back highest point and work around the body. Pivot grading gives an even distribution around the garment block as you continuously move the block around adding in the extra throughout the block (or removing).

Grading a Skirt

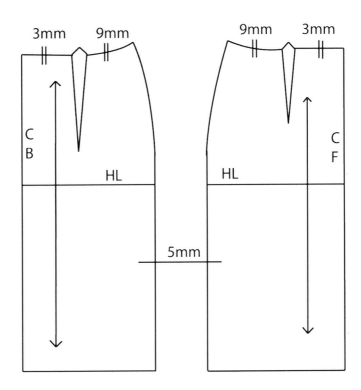

Graded Skirt Example

The example shows the size 10 block graded to a size 12 and a size 14.

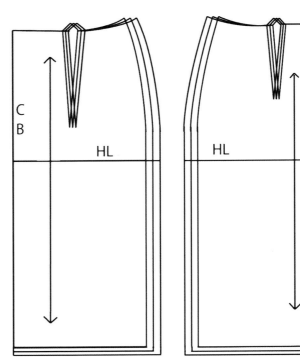

FASHION DESIGN

Grading Trousers

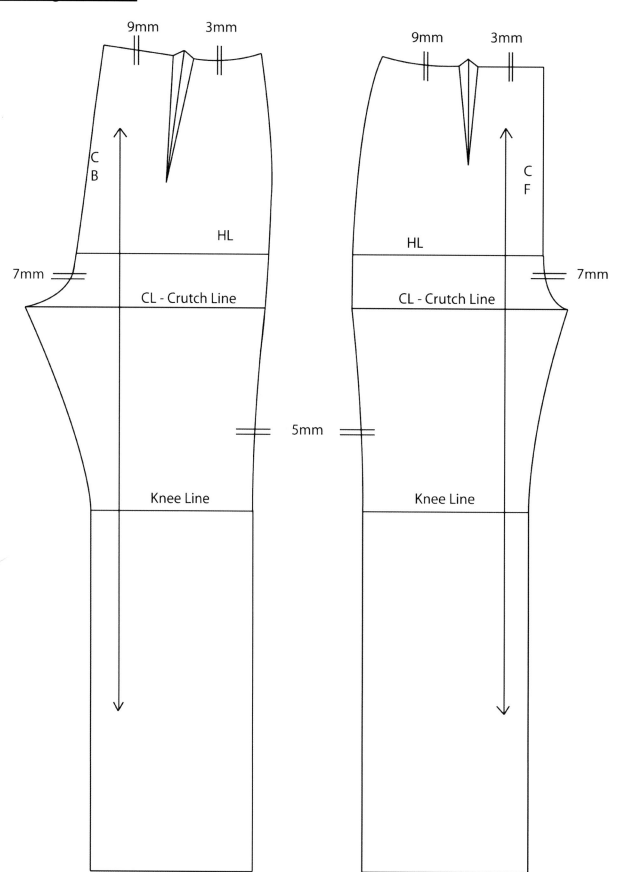

Grading Sleeves

FASHION DESIGN

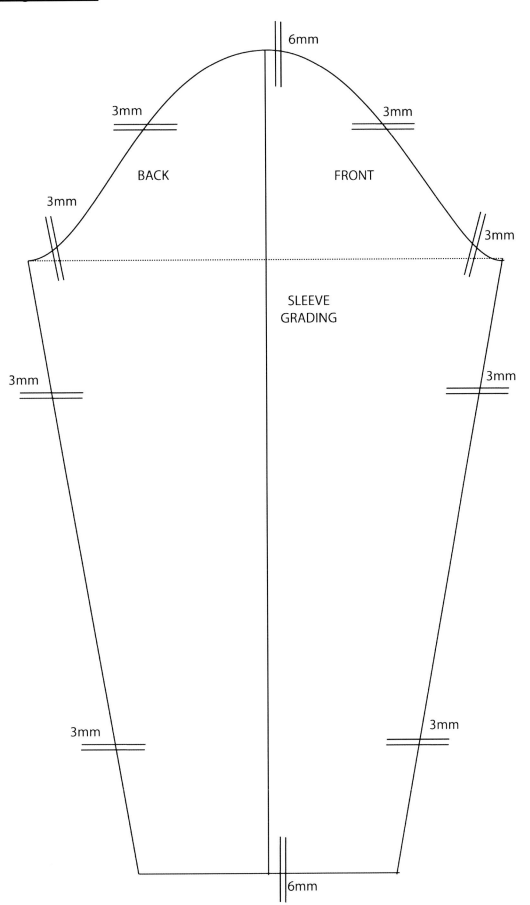

BACK

FRONT

SLEEVE
GRADING

6mm

3mm

3mm

3mm

3mm

3mm

3mm

3mm

3mm

6mm

FASHION DESIGN

Grading Back Bodice

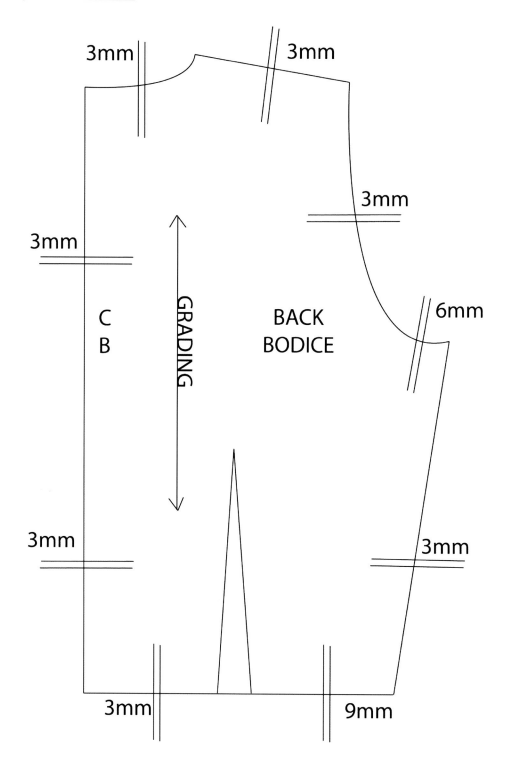

3mm

3mm

3mm

3mm

GRADING

C B

BACK BODICE

6mm

3mm

3mm

9mm

FASHION DESIGN

Grading Front Bodice

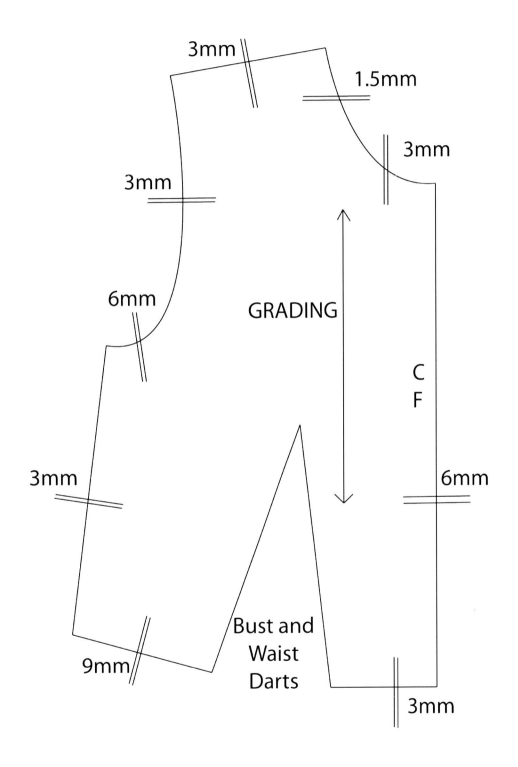

3mm

1.5mm

3mm

3mm

3mm

6mm

GRADING

C
F

3mm

6mm

9mm

Bust and
Waist
Darts

3mm

19. SPECIFICATION TEMPLATES

To draw designs for tailors or factories a technical drawing is required to show clear details of the garment design. Drawing by hand it is advisable to use a specification template. Adobe illustrator is the computer program used in industry for drawing technical specifications.

Technical specification templates are basic symmetrical shapes that can be traced around and adapted into finished design.

Designs should show front, back and any close up detailing to help the factories make your designs. The templates show a top, dress and trousers. The back neck needs to be raised for the back views. These three templates can be used for all garments. Skirts can be designed by tracing around the trouser block, jackets and coats can be designed from the top template.

Be as detailed as possible when drawing technical drawings, showing topstitching detail, keeping the body size as realistic to design - making the body larger for coats, small for bustiers etc.

Style Lines

Topstiching Lines

Zippers

Buttons

Button Holes

Zipper Pulley

Seam lines need to be straight lines
Top stitching lines are dashed
Zippers are horizontal dashed lines
Buttons are circular
Button holes are horizontal dashed lines
Zipper pulleys oblong shape (show these for side zipper placements)

Top Template

FASHION DESIGN

Trouser Template

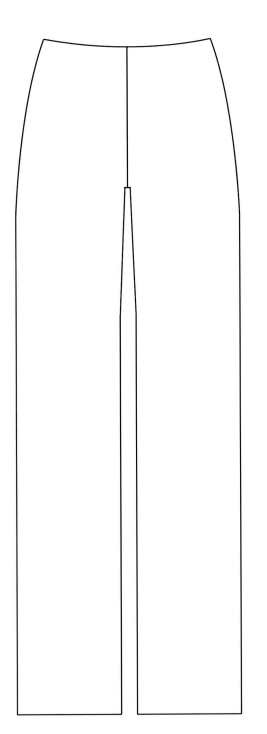

Dress Template

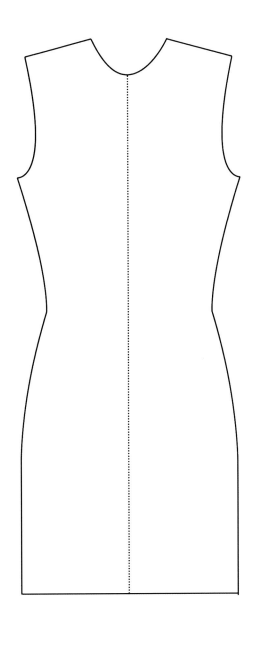

FASH ON DESIGN

20. FABRIC COSTING

Fabric widths

Silk and some cotton fabric are generally 115cm wide. All other fabrics are 150cm wide.
Depending on the width of the fabric will depend on how much is required to make a design.
Also there are one direction fabrics:-

> Corduroy
> Velvet
> Brushed Cotton
> Directional Prints

When using a one directional fabric all patter pieces must be placed facing the same direction.
** We brush DOWN our bodies – so for velvet, corduroy and brushed cotton place the "head" of each pattern piece at the end of the fabric where you would brush down.

For all other fabrics you can place pattern pieces upside down as well as the right way up to achieve a better costing. For some fabrics cross grain can also be used. Cotton works well for cross grain cutting but some other fabrics do not.

Costing a Garment

FABRIC	QUANTITY	PRICE PER UNIT	TOTAL PRICE
Outer Fabric			
2nd Fabric			
3rd Fabric			
Lining			
Interlining			
Thread			
Zipper			
Buttons			
Other:			

FASHION DESIGN

SPECIFICATION SHEET - TOPS, DRESSES

Garment Name

FRONT	BACK

MEASUREMENT	CM'S	FABRIC
BL - Bust Line		
WL - Waist Line		
HL - Hipline		
Hemline		TRIMS
CBL - Centre Back Length		
Shoulder		
Neck opening		
Front neck drop		** Add in additional measurements from design details
Back neck drop		
Bust dart length		
Armhole straight		
Sleeve length		
Bicep		
Sleeve hem		

FINISHING DETAILS

FASHION DESIGN

SPECIFICATION SHEET - JACKETS, COATS

Garment Name

FRONT	BACK

MEASUREMENT	CM'S	FABRIC
BL - Bust Line		
WL - Waist Line		
HL - Hipline		
Hemline		TRIMS
CBL - Centre Back Length		
Back vent length		
Shoulder		
Neck opening		** Add in additional measurements from design details
Breakline length		
Collar width		
Collar height		
Bust dart length		
Armhole straight		
Sleeve length		
Bicep		
Sleevecuff width		
Pocket length		
Pocket flap width		
FINISHING DETAILS		

FASHION DESIGN

SPECIFICATION SHEET - SKIRTS, TROUSERS

Garment Name

FRONT	BACK

MEASUREMENT	CM'S	FABRIC
WL - Waist Line		
HL - Hipline		
Body Rise		
WL to hem		TRIMS
Waistband / Facing height		
Hem width		
		** Add in additional measurements from design details

FINISHING DETAILS

21. FABRICS

Cutting Fabric

Fabric should be folded with the right side inside (the side you want to see when you wear your garment). Join the selvedge edges together (the natural edge of the fabric and not where it has been cut in the shop) and place along a straight edge – the edge of a table.

Pattern pieces should be placed on the fabric in the best possible way to use the least amount of fabric to make your garment. Chalk should be used on heavier fabrics and pins on lightweight fabrics. Pins should only ever be pinned within seam allowances so as not to make a mark on your garment. All notches and drill holes should be marked on fabric when cutting out – either with a pin or with chalk. To lay out all pattern pieces at once not only saves time but also saves fabric.

Fabric Qualities

The same fabric can be used to make a multitude of designs. A circle skirt can be made in any fabric from silk chiffon, which is very fine and drapes well to a coarse linen. The same pattern can be used for both styles. The difference is how the finished garment will look. One will be soft and flowing, the other a firmer shape.

The key thing to consider is what the fabric is like. The thinner the fabric the more it will drape, the thicker the fabric the stiffer the design will be. Fine fabrics like chiffon do not work very well in tailored garments. Stiff fabrics like taffeta do not drape so would not work in draped blouses or dress designs.

Certain fabrics also are predominantly used in different seasons and garments. Linen is only used in the summer for its lightweight and fiber properties, which do not keep you warm in colder climates. Wool suiting can be used all seasons, but heavier wool fabrics would only be used in the winter, as they are warm fabrics. Cotton is known as a casual fabric, but cotton blends can be used for
eveningwear. Silk is predominantly used for eveningwear because of it is expense. It is however a very versatile fiber that can be tailored, draped and molded.

Jersey fabrics are used for t-shirts, basic camisoles, vests etc and are seen all year round. A common jersey is 95% cotton and 5% lycra. There are now many types of man made jersey fabrics used in all garment classifications, from heavy to light weight. Most jersey fabrics have a good drape. Jersey fabric comes in different weights and can also be used for eveningwear designs.

Knitwear is known for its warmth and is predominantly a winter yarn. However fine cotton yarns are used in the summer for cardigans and lightweight jumpers. Crochet is an open form of knitting and is also made by yarn and is therefore classed as knitwear. Knitwear works well in a variety of tops, jumpers and cardigans but is also used for dresses. The way knitwear is made it is more open and unstable so can go out of shape quickly when used in fitted styles.

FASHION DESIGN

Fabric are classified into three groups:-

Woven fabrics

Made on a loom with a warp and weft. Generally with no stretch although some woven fabrics have elastane or lycra sewn into it to give limited stretch. Woven fabrics are widely used in the fashion industry, from denim jeans to cotton blouses. The four natural fibers, silk, wool, cotton and linen are made into many different qualities of woven fabrics, either by themselves or combined with another fiber. Man-made fibers are also used in woven fabrics from polyster, either by itself or blended with cotton and other natural fibers. Technology of man made fibers is continuously evolving and many new fabrics continue to enter the market place.

Jersey fabrics

Made on a circular machine. Jersey wear is T-shirts, swimwear, most underwear, leggings etc. Always stretchable but not always made with elastane or lycra.

Jersey fabrics are made of natural fibers and man made fibers, pure or mixed. From very light weight to heavy, which can be used for dresses and eveningwear. Jersey garments are made from a different set of basic blocks, which have no body shaping (darts) as the fabric stretches over the body.

Knitwear

Hand knitwear is made with knitting needles. However most knitwear is made on knitting machines. It is made with yarn sewn together – not yardage of fabric.

Hand knitting and machine can also be designed into patterns and shapes - crochet, tatting, ribbing etc.

FASHION DESIGN

	NATURAL FIBERS
SILK	Measured by weight in "MM"
Organza	A sheer silk with highly twisted threads, which make it strong and crisp. Has a natural sheen.
Satin	Shinny one-sided surface. Comes in lightweight to heavier weight varieties. Satin has a nice drape. Duchess Satin is heaviest and much stiffer in hand feel.
Chiffon	Often the lightest weight and most diaphanous of the silks, Chiffon is also the most see-through. It creates the "billows" of fabric that add dimension to garments. 8mm – 12mm
Georgette	Georgette is heavier chiffon. Over 12mm would be classed as georgette.
Habotai	Habotai is a lightweight, sheer, plain weave fabric. It is one of the less expensive and more commonly available silk fabrics. Habotai can often be found as light as 5 mm. Often used as lining as it is firm. However often found with sand washing treatments, which make it a desirable women's wear evening fabric.
Crepe de Chine	Crepe de chine is a lightweight fabric made by twisting some fibers clockwise and others counterclockwise. The twisted fibers are then woven in a plain-weave fabric, but it's the twisted fibers, not the weave, that gives crepe its distinctive "pebbly" look and feel rather than a shiny luster. Both sides of the fabric look and feel the same. Crepe de chine doesn't ravel as easily as other silk fabrics, but it will tear if not handled gently.
Charmeuse	The back of the fabric is a flattened crepe while the front is a shimmery satin weave. Charmeuse has even more drape than crepe de chine and works well for scarves, blouses and lingerie.
Jacquard	Jacquard silks offer various woven patterns, using matte and reflective threads to create a light and dark effect in the fabric. This effect is similar to brocade, although the Jacquard is originally created in one color. These are generally heavier weight and more densely woven.
Dupioni	Dupioni is a plain-weave fabric with slubbed ribs. It has a stiff, taffeta-like hand and is usually dyed in bright colors. The fabric doesn't stand up well to stress and ravels easily. Washing will make the fabric lose some of its stiffness, and the color will soften as the excess dye is washed away.
Noil	Silk noil is made from the short fibers left after combing and carding so it doesn't shine like many other silk fabrics. Noil looks similar to cotton, but has the soft feel of silk against the skin. It also drapes better than cotton and resists wrinkling. It can be machine washed on gentle and dried on low, but this will cause a faded, "weathered" look.
Raw silk	Raw silk is any silk yarn or fabric that hasn't had the sericin - the natural "gum" that protects the fiber - removed. The fabric is stiff and dull and the sericin tends to attract dirt and odors. Common in Indian silks.
Tussah	Tussah silk, often called shantung, is made from the cocoons of wild tussah silk worms who eat oak and juniper leaves – their "natural" food. Because the worm isn't grown in a controlled environment, the moth hatches from the cocoon thus interrupting the filament length and making the fibers short and coarse instead of long and lustrous. Tussah silk is difficult to dye and to most often available in its natural color, a creamy tan.
Shantung	Once made from hand-reeled tussah silk, today's shantung is usually made with cultivated silk warp yarns and heavier dupioni filling yarns. Depending

WOOL	
Alpaca	Domestic camel hair, a fine and silky yarn
Angora	Wool yarn from a goat. Long and lustrous
Cashmere	Combed from the fleece of a goat. Used for knit and woven
Suiting	Comes in summer and winter weights. Woven into twills and plain weaves. Used for men's and women's suits.
Crepe	Crepe is made by twisting some fibers clockwise and others counterclockwise. The twisted fibers are then woven in a plain-weave fabric, but it's the twisted fibers, not the weave, that gives crepe its distinctive "pebbly" look and feel rather than a shiny luster. Both sides of the fabric look and feel the same
Tartan	A woollen, twill weave fabric in multicoloured plaid designs – the heritage is from Scottish Clans.
Tweed	Tweed is woven wool in a variety of colours and patterns - checks etc
Mohair	The hair of the angora goat. Has a natural luster and wears well.
Melton	Felted wool. Generally used on the inside of tailored jackets. Although a very dense wool it is suitable for winter coats
Brushed	Woven wool where needles have torn the filaments to create a soft smooth shinny effect – "brushed". One way is soft; the other going against the needles is not so smooth.
Camel	Very soft hand feels warm wool used for coats.
COTTON	
Broderie Anglaise	An embroidered small pattern design with holes cut out
Canvas	A firm closely woven plain weave cloth. Very strong.
Corduroy	A cotton fabric woven with a pile, which is then cut into stripes or checks to create the corduroy. From needle cord to jumbo cord.
Chambray	Closely woven, smooth and strong.
Denim	A heavy weight cotton constructed in a twill weave
Gingham	A woven check cotton fabric. The checks ranging from very small to very big.
Pique	Has raised small "spots" like a dobby design and look
Sateen	Shinny on one side giving the look of satin
Shirting	A fine cotton can be found in plain and twill weaves. Traditionally used for men's tailored shirts. Often blended with polyester
Twill	Twill is a type of weave where the grain runs a/symmetric down the length of the fabric
Velvet	A close woven fabric with a short dense pile, soft and rich in texture
Voile	A very fine cotton
Seersucker	A thin "puckered" fabric in striped or checked designs. The puckering raises part of the fabric.
Lawn	A plain weave using high yarn counts to give a silky hand feel and finish
LINEN	
Linen	A crisp fabric woven from the flax plant. Blended with cotton for a softer hand feel.
Hemp	Hemp is a plant, the fibres of which are woven together to create hemp - a cheaper linen
Flax	The flax plant makes linen. The fibres of the plant are treated and woven together.

MANUFACTURED FIBERS	
Nylon	Synthetic fiber consisting of chemical units linked by amide groups. A light, strong, resilient fiber with good resistance to abrasion. Can be washed and drip-dried easily, need little or no ironing. Can be permanently pleated, tends to build up static electricity and attracts dirt but resists stains well. Often used in blends and gives strength and resistance to wear.
Polyester	Synthetic fiber consisting of chemical units linked by ester groups. A light strong fiber with good resistance to abrasion and creasing. Can be washed and drip-dried easily. Can be permanently pleated. Tends to build up static electricity and attracts dirt. Resists stains well except oil. Often used in blends to increase strength and resistance to wear. Often blended with cotton.
Acetate	Man made fiber consisting of cellulose acetate. Not very strong, poor abrasion resistance, creases easily. Has a good drape and silky hand feel. Highly flammable. Heat sensitive and can melt under a hot iron. Fading of colour problems. High luster and smooth texture. Dry-clean recommended. Weaker when wet.
Rayon	The first manufactured cellulosic fiber. Always blended with other fabrics such as cotton. Filaments are circular, serrated. Highly absorbent, soft, comfortable, easy to dry and versatile. Rayon has a soft drape. Very adaptable fiber and can be used to copy the features of many different fibers.
Acrylic	Synthetic fiber consisting of at least 85% by mass of acrylonitrile units linked together. Light, fairly strong and durable. Resists sunlight. Does not crease easily, highly flammable, sensitive to heat and can be damaged by hot irons. Easy to wash and drip dry. Resembles wool in appearance and handle. Warm without being heavy. Colder to touch than wool.
Viscose	Man made fiber consisting of regenerated cellulose. Resembles cotton but not as strong or durable. Creases easily, highly flammable. Often used in blends with other fibers.

FASHION DESIGN

FASHION DESIGN